The Financial Times Essential Guide to
Leading Your Team

The Financial Times Essential Guide to Leading Your Team

How to set goals, measure performance and reward talent

Graham Yemm

Harlow, England • London • New York • Boston • San Francisco • Toronto • Sydney
Auckland • Singapore • Hong Kong • Tokyo • Seoul • Taipei • New Delhi
Cape Town • São Paulo • Mexico City • Madrid • Amsterdam • Munich • Paris • Milan

PEARSON EDUCATION LIMITED
Edinburgh Gate
Harlow CM20 2JE
United Kingdom
Tel: +44 (0)1279 623623
Fax: +44 (0)1279 431059
Web: www.pearson.com/uk

First published 2012 (print and electronic)

Pearson Education is not responsible for the content of third-party internet sites.

ISBN: 978-0-273-77242-2 (print)
ISBN: 978-0-273-77243-9 (PDF)
ISBN: 978-0-273-77244-6 (ePub)

British Library Cataloguing-in-Publication Data
A catalogue record for this book is available from the British Library

Library of Congress Cataloging-in-Publication Data
Yemm, Graham.
 The Financial Times essential guide to leading your team : how to set goals, measure performance and reward talent / Graham Yemm.
    p. cm. -- (Financial Times essential guides)
 Includes index.
 ISBN 978-0-273-77242-2 (pbk.)
 1. Teams in the workplace. 2. Leadership. I. Title. II. Title: Essential guide to leading your team.
 HD66.Y46 2012
 658.4'022--dc23
                    2012029253

ARP Impression 98

Printed edition typeset in 8.75/12pt Stone serif by 30
Printed in Great Britain by Clays Ltd, St Ives plc

Contents

Acknowledgements

We are grateful to the following for permission to reproduce copyright material:

Figures 4.2 and 10.2 and the tables on pp.46–7 from Adair, J., *Action-Centred Leadership* (Gower Publishing, 1979). This material appears by kind permission of John Adair.

In some instances we were unable to trace the owners of copyright material, and we would appreciate any information that would enable us to do so.

Introduction

Throughout your life you will have been exposed to a number of leaders. You have possibly had situations where you have been leading others. Many of these could have been with formal roles or titles, others where the leadership role has been taken (or given) informally. We have had these experiences throughout our childhood and school days until the present. Some of them will have been positive and successful, others might have been the opposite! We do not always know or understand why this is the case; however, we do know whether it is working or not.

Leadership and team working are all around us and key to our work environment and yet they are tricky to recognise or define. This does not make them any less important. Within the workplace, being able to get teams (and groups) to improve performance is vital for success.

In this guide I will help you to:

- recognise the benefits of understanding the background to teambuilding and team working;
- learn how you can be a confident leader;
- understand why it is powerful to be able to adapt your leadership to fit with the needs of individuals and the team;
- learn how to use a number of specific tools and techniques to use with your team to produce more effective performance and outcomes.

Why should you work through the book?

A few years ago I was involved with a series of training programmes with a large bank. We worked with a number of their managers on their teambuilding, leadership and communication skills. When we went back to review progress over three and then six months the participants reported a 73 per cent improvement in their understanding of their role as a team leader, and a 61 per cent lift in their ability as a team leader.

More importantly this was the difference to the business and within the branches:

> *Well over budget – already achieved year's targets (three months early!). More focus on end results and monitoring of performance – making the group feel they are one team – deal with problems in a positive and constructive way – encourage more participation and sharing ideas – better communication within team, with colleagues – understand my team's needs better – make the best of each individual – focus on keeping team spirit high – make the group feel they are one team – all go in the same direction – get things done through others – express myself clearly and point out the roles to every team member – get tangible achievements – work with others instead of ordering them – praise and motivate – involve in decisions – confront the problems faced with some team members in a more positive way – team is more results oriented – every member's role is as important as the leader's.*

These outcomes are the result of understanding the concepts of leadership and teambuilding, practising them and constantly applying them. They can deliver results such as those reported by the client's managers. You too can have these!

In each chapter I will give you the knowledge for the particular subject, frequently with self-assessment or raising self-awareness; thinking about the people you need to lead and assessing them; and moving on to specific tools and techniques which you can apply. I have included a number of areas with small checklists or coaching questions to encourage you to take these ideas on board and build them into your day-to-day work.

The first part of the book will look at the fundamentals of teams and teambuilding, leadership and management. You will understand how to identify at which stage your team is at within a group dynamics model and how to help them to move forward within that process to become a high-performing team. You will appreciate why you need to have a variety of different characters and personalities in your team in order to get the best performance from them, balancing their roles. You will be able to look at your team members and identify their preferred team roles, and your own. We will introduce you to two specific leadership approaches and show you how to apply them with your team.

The next part will introduce you to a number of specific methods and tools to use with your team. These will help you to generate effective teamwork and performance from the people in your team. You will become more confident as a leader and your team will feel more comfortable following you because you are acting more competently and professionally. Each chapter will focus on a particular set of tools or skills. I will cover the basic principles and then give ideas for how to apply them and encourage you to develop your own plans for using them with your teams.

The final stage will bring all of these elements together. You will get maximum value from working through the different activities to help you reinforce your learning and, more importantly, identifying how you will start to implement the key messages in your work and with your teams. I want it to be practical and supportive for you.

Planning

1

Facing the challenges of leading your team

When you have any level of management or supervisory role it is usually presumed that you will be comfortable leading people and know how to create teams. If only it were that easy!

Can you remember how you felt when you were given your first position where you were responsible for managing and leading others? Probably a mix of excitement and apprehension as you looked forward to the challenge. Happy that you had been given the role and that someone felt you were capable of doing it. Then the realisation dawns, the job requires a whole range of skills which you are not sure you possess.

When we look at why many promotions occur we can begin to understand why this is the feeling. Figure 1.1 illustrates the typical process. The more senior the role the greater the amount of 'managing' involved, and moving down through middle management to the more junior or supervisory positions, the balance moves towards more 'doing', although not totally.

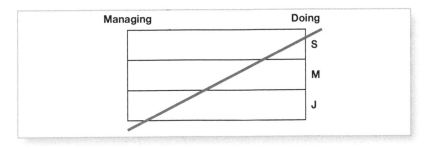

figure 1.1   The promotion problem

However, if we think about why many people are promoted it is because they demonstrate their capability at 'doing' and they are moved into a position which requires less of that and more 'managing'. (I do recognise that the more enlightened organisations take a rounded view of this and consider whether the person has the qualities to manage and lead, possibly checking them through interviews or assessment centres.) There you are in your new role with these different responsibilities, with people to lead, frequently with very little training or guidance and trying not to show your lack of confidence. You want to convince others that you are capable. So, what do you do? Revert to your comfort zone and stick with 'doing' rather than 'managing'. This can cause various problems which you may recognise. These include: you need to work longer hours; your focus is on tasks rather than your people; issues with motivation; you are perceived to be interfering or not delegating; your people are not being developed.

Management is about getting things done. It requires coordination of resources to achieve a defined end result (objective or target) with and through people. It is the science of continuous improvement.

Management is the effective use of resources to achieve organisational goals.

Most organisations will state that their most important resource or asset is their people. As a manager, you also have a variety of additional resources: money, equipment, technology, plant, stock, premises, etc. On a personal level you have your own knowledge and time. Ask yourself how you can split your time across all of these resources. Which one can actually improve performance and productivity? Yes, people. How much time do you spend focusing on your people, thinking about them, communicating with them, developing them? Why is this? If you are like the vast majority of managers I have come across, the balance is usually weighted significantly towards the more operational type of resources and the people are something of an afterthought.

In today's business and economic climate it is even more important to be able to get the most from your people. Financial constraints and challenges mean that most of you have to achieve more with either the same number of people or fewer. Therefore, getting more from your team is essential.

Arguably, management is something which is straightforward and the various tasks required can be learned and developed. It is also easier to find things to do within these tasks and to feel as though you are being productive. Leadership and dealing with people are more imprecise and contain a lot of variables. In this book I will help you understand the key principles and skills of leadership and how to apply them with your people to enable them to be successful.

You will recognise the elements involved in building a team and making sure it continues to function as a team. I will show you how to apply them to your own situation and what to do to keep the team developing and improving performance. You will be able to work with both individuals and the team to get their commitment and maximise their contribution. As you work through the book you will cover a range of key skills to help you to become a more productive team leader and to feel more confident in your role, now and in the future.

To help you think about what you would like to learn from this book, have a go at this small test. Read each statement or question in the table below and assess your current level of skill or knowledge for it.

0–1   Don't know, no real knowledge, don't do this.

2–3   Some awareness, some knowledge, do sometimes, could be better.

4–5   Comfortable with this, think I am competent or good at it (though not complacent!).

When you have scored each group of statements/questions, identify some specific action or outcome you want to achieve for it. Pay particular attention to those items which you have scored between 0 and 3.

No.	Item	Rating	Notes
1	How well do you know the characteristics of an effective team?		
2	Can you describe what types of team you need to set up and lead?		
3	Are you able to recognise the different stages a team goes through as it develops?		

Objective/action:

4	What types of roles are required for a well-balanced team?		
5	Can you identify the preferred roles of your team members?		
6	How well do you recognise the benefits of having differences among the team members and their styles, rather than too much similarity?		

Objective/action:

▷

No.	Item	Rating	Notes
7	How comfortable are you with leading people?		
8	Do you feel you should change your leadership style with your team?		
9	Do you understand your role and responsibilities as a leader?		

Objective/action:

No.	Item	Rating	Notes
10	How important is it for the team to have clear goals?		
11	Do you make sure individuals have their own goals to achieve?		
12	Can you identify areas to set standards of performance or key performance indicators?		

Objective/action:

No.	Item	Rating	Notes
13	Do you have processes or systems in place for monitoring the team's performance?		
14	Are you willing to act quickly when you see things slipping (collectively or with individuals)?		
15	What could you do to involve the team members in monitoring performance? Would you be happy to do so?		

Objective/action:

No.	Item	Rating	Notes
16	How well do you feel you communicate with the team?		
17	How comfortable are you dealing with people face to face?		
18	Could you improve communication within the team?		

Objective/action:

No.	Item	Rating	Notes
19	Do you consciously look for opportunities to delegate to team members and to develop their skills?		
20	How good are you at 'catching 'em doing something right' and giving praise?		
21	Do you know what type of recognition or acknowledgement will work best for each of your team members?		

Objective/action:

No.	Item	Rating	Notes
22	Do you prefer to avoid or prevent conflict within the team?		
23	How well do you understand the dangers of 'groupthink'?		
24	How comfortable are you at addressing and handling conflict within the team?		

Objective/action:

Look at your objectives or actions and list them on a sheet of paper. Take the opportunity to expand on each one and add more detail if it helps. As you read each of the chapters that follow, you will find information and ideas to help you achieve these objectives. You do not have to go through them in the order they appear in the table. If you would prefer to prioritise them differently and work through the book in that sequence that is fine.

To summarise the differences between management and leadership:

The Manager	The Leader
Administers	*Innovates*
Is a copy	*Is an original*
Maintains	*Develops*
Focuses on systems	*Focuses on people*
Relies on control	*Inspires trust*
Short-range view	*Long-range view*
Asks how and when	*Asks what and why*
Eye on the bottom-line	*Eye on the horizon*
Imitates	*Originates*
Accepts the status quo	*Challenges the status quo*
Obeys orders without question	*Obeys when appropriate – but thinks*
Does things right	*Does the right things*
Is trained	*Learns*
Managers operate within the culture	***Leaders create the culture***

Source: With acknowledgement to Warren Bennis, from his book *On Becoming a Leader*

As you progress through the book you will see how the really effective manager and leader is able to combine many of these characteristics to get the most from their principal resource – their people – especially when they are working in teams.

Summary

- Think about how you spend your time. Are you giving enough to your people so that you can get to know and understand them better?

- Recognise that you need to lead your team and become comfortable in that role.

- Look at the comparison between a manager and a leader and think about what you can do more of in the leader's column to improve your ability.

- Think about the items you scored between 0 and 3 in the assessment exercise. What actions will you take for each of them?

2

What is a team?

In this chapter we will explore a number of aspects of teams and the various types of team you might need to lead. You will recognise the difference between a team and a group and understand why it is helpful for you to do so. I will explain the group dynamics process which occurs as any group or team is being set up and works together. You will be able to use this knowledge to adapt your style and approach according to which stage the team has reached to improve your effectiveness as their leader.

One of the biggest mistakes many managers and leaders make is to use the term 'team' when they are actually referring to a 'group'. This is not just a semantic issue. There are some significant differences between the two and it is important to recognise whether you are leading a group or a team. Having said that, much of what is covered in this book will be useful to you in either situation.

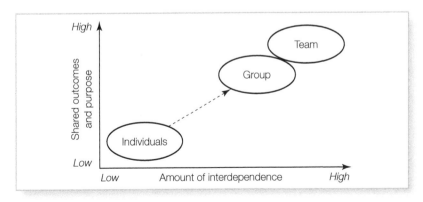

figure 2.1 The differences between a group and a team

Within the workplace there are a number of functions or departments which operate as groups, yet are frequently referred to as teams. Sales is a great example of this. Many organisations talk about their sales team, or the customer support or service team. The reality is that in the majority of cases these are groups, because the individuals work towards their own targets or objectives. They do not share these with others (except in rare cases of team selling or dedicated account teams) and so are independent and have sole accountability for their own results and performance. To call a group a team does not make them a team; wishing for them to work as a team doesn't work either. Think about what other functions in your organisation might be groups rather than teams.

There are a number of definitions of teams. The common elements are that they are a *small number* of people (up to a maximum of 12 and often fewer), with *complementary skills* who *work together* to achieve a *common purpose*, and who are *collectively accountable*.

Generally, teams will be more productive and successful than groups, but not always. A well-led and well-run group can still be very efficient and effective without being changed into a team. If it is right for the organisation and the people, keep it as it is!

The group dynamics process – Tuckman[1]

When you bring a number of individuals together to operate as a team or a group, they do not start off as a highly productive unit. They will go through a process of development involving a series of stages. Some progress through these rapidly and others never develop beyond a particular stage. The role of the leader plays a significant part in this. There are four broad stages through which teams develop; although they could be seen as discrete there is often overlap between one stage and another.

These four broad stages, as proposed by Bruce Tuckman in 1965, are: forming, storming, norming and performing. Tuckman later added a fifth stage: disintegrating (see Figure 2.2 and table).

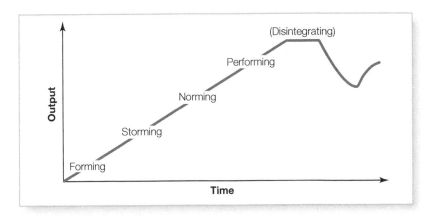

figure 2.2 The group dynamics process

STAGE I – TESTING (FORMING)	STAGE II – CONFUSION (STORMING)
CHARACTERISTICS	CHARACTERISTICS
▪ Polite	▪ Cliques start to have influence
▪ Dependence on leader	▪ Conflicts occur
▪ Guarding	▪ People confronted
▪ Watchful	▪ Hidden agendas begin to be raised
▪ Impersonal	▪ Struggle for leadership by cliques
▪ No conflicts	▪ Opting out
▪ Need for group identity is low	▪ Feeling stuck
▪ Concern for structure, methods, etc.	▪ Own positions rationalised
▪ Hidden agendas stay hidden	▪ Lack of listening

STAGE III – GETTING ORGANISED (NORMING)	STAGE IV – MATURE CLOSENESS (PERFORMING)
CHARACTERISTICS	CHARACTERISTICS
▪ Procedures developed	▪ Resourcefulness
▪ Issues confronted	▪ Creativity
▪ More open exchange of ideas and views	▪ Flexible
▪ Cliques dissolved	▪ Open
▪ Leadership shared	▪ Effective
▪ More listening and co-operation	▪ Close and supportive
▪ Giving feedback	▪ Settled independence
▪ Pre-conceived ideas are changed	▪ High group morale
▪ Creativity high	▪ Warmth/closeness of members
	▪ Empathy
	▪ High level of problem-solving behaviour

Source: Table and figure from Tuckman, B., 'Development sequence in small groups', *Psychological Bulletin* (American Psychological Association, 1965).

Exercise

Where do you think your team is within the stages of team development?

What evidence do you have for reaching this conclusion?

What can you do to help them move through towards the top?

It is important to understand this process because it happens to every group or team. Many never make it to the 'norming' or 'performing' stages, often as a result of their manager blocking their progress. Think about groups and teams you have been part of, whether in work or outside, and you will probably be able to identify times when you have been at the different stages.

You can play a key role in facilitating the progress through these steps by understanding where the team is and adapting your style and approach to suit their needs.

Forming

The group need the leader to provide a lot of guidance and direction. They will want you to provide clear outcomes and aims, be specific about individual roles and responsibilities, establish the processes and explain 'how' the team will work. Individuals may be cautious about opening up or expressing their thoughts or concerns. They prefer to be guarded until they feel more comfortable with their colleagues. As the leader you need to be visible and approachable to deal with questions and to show your interest and commitment.

Storming

This step can be uncomfortable for the leader for a variety of reasons. It is also the step where many leaders unintentionally block progress. The team members are aiming to sort out their own positions in relation to others. Sub-groups and cliques might form, leading to challenges within the team and towards you as the leader. Some leaders see this apparent turbulence and think it is not a good thing, so they work hard to quash it and to prevent any conflict. Unfortunately, this holds the output level down! This is a necessary part of the team development process, a bit like going through adolescence. You can help move things forward by keeping the team focused on their goals and outputs, and by keeping discussions objective about performance or behaviour. Accept that there might be times when the team decide you are to be the target for their frustration or concerns. Allow this to happen and move their focus on to how they want things to be in the future and how they can contribute to achieving this. Your role is to coach and encourage and move them forward rather than becoming stuck in the present or past.

Norming

This is something of a breakthrough stage. The team members are clear about their roles and responsibilities and feel a sense of commitment to the overall outcome and purpose of the team. They are establishing a greater sense of identity, belonging and shared values. The challenge for you as the leader is to let go of much of the directing and become more of a facilitator and enabler. The team will be developing its own processes and ways of working and will be open to more delegation from you.

Performing

By now the team know what it is doing, why it is doing it and how it will do it. Their focus is on their performance and achievement of stretching goals. They handle disagreements and conflict positively and constructively. At the same time they will work at supporting and encouraging each other. Your role is to provide the overall direction, projects where appropriate, encouragement and development opportunities for individuals. Be available for advice and help if required.

Disintegrating (sometimes seen as adjourning)

Eventually the team will come to an end. The project or task is completed, some people leave or some new ones arrive. At this stage, look for an opportunity to reflect on what has gone well, celebrate success.

Thank the team members for what they have contributed and reflect on lessons learned. As this happens, plan for change as you move to a new team, new projects or whatever new structure you have to lead. Recognise that the new team (even if it is only slightly changed) will still go through the group dynamics model – although it will start from a higher base on the outputs and will hopefully move up the stages more quickly!

Case study

A research and development department within a small, specialist bio-tech company was expanding rapidly. They promoted James to a management role where he was in charge of about half of the people in the department. Prior to this, for eight months, he had been one of the development scientists. Several new employees joined as part of the section he was running. He was excited about the opportunity but also apprehensive as it was his first management or supervisory role.

James had been briefed by his director about the role and given a number of targets to be achieved. James had met with each of the team members individually to get to know them and explain what he wanted from them, and he held several meetings with the whole team to share ideas and update progress. Initially, things seemed to be going well and James felt positive and that he was doing the right thing.

However, by the time of the third meeting he noticed that maybe all was not running smoothly. When he asked for input from the team members some were quiet, others were critical of things and blaming colleagues or the company. The overall atmosphere was unpleasant and uncomfortable. James was not happy and felt he needed to step in to stop the blame and criticism and he stressed the need for people to work together and not to create conflict. As the meeting finished and people left there was some muttering and moaning, but he felt he had controlled it just in time.

Over the next few days James noticed that the mood was still subdued and small cliques had formed. He tried spending time with individuals and checking that all was OK. He heard mixed messages, some still moaning and others claiming things were 'fine'. By the next team meeting, the following week, if anything the atmosphere was worse. James decided he had to stop this, so he told the team that they had to work together and co-operate. Nothing seemed to change and the overall performance was beginning to suffer. To make matters worse he started to hear rumours that some of the team members, both old and new, were talking of leaving the company.

James plucked up the courage to go and talk to the director and to ask for some help or ideas. He was sure he was doing the right thing to try to stop the conflict and friction between the team members. The director let him finish and then surprised James in several ways. He explained how something similar had happened to him when he started in management and he had been through the same feelings as James. The director pulled a binder from a bookcase in his office and opened it to show James the diagram of the group dynamics process. He told him about the stages – especially 'storming' – and how uncomfortable it could be for all concerned. The director surprised James when he told him how he dealt with it. James listened and agreed to give it a go.

The next team meeting started as scheduled. The atmosphere was still not positive. James, sensing this, drew a deep breath and told the team he was not happy about their on-going niggling and criticising and their reluctance to work together. People were shocked and some looked ready to argue back, others looked sulky and a few just seemed to withdraw into themselves. He then took them by surprise when he said that for the next 30 minutes they would have the opportunity to get all moans out in the open, explain what they were unhappy with and why, and (most importantly) say what they wanted and how the team could work to achieve this – and what would happen when they did.

James sat back and listened; he allowed the team to do the talking and he only became involved to write the goals and plans for the future on to the flipchart. At the end of the 30 minutes he called a halt and went back to the agenda for the meeting. Although it still took a couple more meetings and weeks to really come together, the team was through the 'storming' stage and started moving forward.

Types of team

There are a number of types of team which you might have in organisations and need to lead. The most common are as follows.

Work teams

These are typically job specific within a department or function. They can be long lasting but evolving as new people come into the work area or others move on. They will meet more regularly and much of their time will be spent exploring elements of their own work or processes. Over time they can move to becoming increasingly self-managing and more delegation is possible.

Project teams

These are made up of members from different areas of the business, depending on the specific skills or knowledge needed. They will usually have a particular project to work through and deliver using a disciplined approach. The project team needs to be kept reasonably small, or broken into smaller sub-teams, to address specific tasks. The project team needs a good balance of leadership and management skills from you in order to keep on top of the plan and schedule, while you need to be influencing and engaging the team members as they will often have conflicting demands on their time and energy. A challenge leading these teams is that you often have little or no direct authority over some of the team members and need to use your influencing skills.

Focus teams

This team is created to address or focus on a specific area or issue. They may be problem solving, looking into a particular improvement area, or similar. They will be looking to generate ideas to improve parts of the business or introduce changes. Typically, they will have a clear remit and be working to a clear timescale – with small numbers. Depending on the experience of the team members, the leader can move from being directive, to facilitating, to encouraging contribution and progress.

Virtual teams

As the name suggests, these teams have little or no direct personal contact. (In extremes the team members may be on different continents!) The team may be touching in to all of the other three, and almost certainly is a work team. The improvements in technology combined with moves towards remote working make these a growing form of team. To become effective the remote teams need the leader to set a good example with their communication and relationship building. Once things are underway, there is scope to let go and share some of the leadership and responsibility in a similar way to the work teams.

Type of team

	Work	Project	Focus	Virtual
Nature or structure of team	Permanent teams within a function or operation	Brought together to work on specific project	Usually cross-functional, addressing specific business issue or problem	Can be functional or cross-functional – working remotely, often 'knowledge'-based workers
Guide for contact	Meet frequently – even daily	According to schedule for project	Can vary from weekly to every four weeks	Ideally weekly, and possibly more frequent, informal contact
Purpose of contact	Meetings to update, inform, suggest	Briefing, reviewing, action planning	Reporting on actions, planning next steps	Updating, sharing, planning
Purpose of team	Team is given goals and objectives to accomplish along with how much decision-making power they have and when they must consult management. Generally looking at work or process improvements	Defined project to complete or deliver. Each team member will be required to carry out certain work assignments according to their expertise, skill level, desire to learn or area of influence	Team may be permanent or temporary depending on design and required activity, which is typically to focus on implementing an organisational change effort or improving a common process or system	Many similar characteristics with work teams – main difference is geography

	Work	Project	Focus	Virtual
Realities of working together	Greater understanding of joint work promotes new suggestions and idea sharing	There may be conflicts of interest since members could be from different work areas and will have both the project leader and their regular manager to report to as well as receive assignments from, with differing time pressures and priorities Requires high levels of trust, participation, respect and communication among members to accomplish tasks and solve problems	Members come from various departments, where each department holds a part of the overall process. Takes time for relationships to build It may take a while to be productive since there may be problems with communication and trust as departments may have blamed each other for problems in the past or do not understand the work of others on team	Some members will be more proactive and need more contact. Leader needs to be aware of those who seem to be happy to stay on the fringes. Challenge can be to develop broad relationships and not have tight cliques. Care needed not to let some become isolated and feel ignored
Potential for progress	Quick process changes, effective problem solving and fast procedure updates are possible Improvements in efficiency and productivity can be made easily. Easy to implement since group does similar work and may already know each other	Team should work internally within for group decision making, but may work with those outside the team for suggestions or ideas for the team to consider. This can improve the quality of ideas and help the project	Significant process improvements and increased customer satisfaction may result from joint work efforts across different functions	Having shared experiences and knowledge, ideas can be generated quickly and implemented too

Additional benefits	Increased employee involvement and high levels of horizontal communication to better resolve issues and service customers	Success with projects, or even progress towards it, can improve morale of the team and also of the other departments or functions impacted	Acceptance of improvements suggested by team may be better from others outside the team as they were given input to the process through their representative on the team	Economical as unnecessary overheads are not incurred. Also, time efficient as no travel required. Technology is improving all of the time
Role of leader	Provide initial direction, goals and structure. Can then ease back to encourage more of a self-management style as the team becomes more settled	Need to set the overall plan in place and then make sure the team members stick to commitments. Structure means you need to use a lot of influence with team members and colleagues as you rarely have direct authority over all of them	Keep the team focused on deliverables and achievement. Provide clear performance indicators and encourage sharing of ideas and successes back into the organisation or system	Provide the structure and establish the roles and rules for contribution and communication. Once things are underway, can let go and encourage more self-management – though stay aware of involvement levels

Exercise: Characteristics of an effective team

Think about some of the teams you have been part of. Some were probably not so great, and others were successful and you felt good and proud to be part of them.

Start with some of the less successful experiences.

What are the top three reasons you can think of which caused you to remember the time this way?

1

2

3

Let's look on the positive side now. Think about some teams you have been part of which you look back on with pride and a sense of achievement. What do you feel were the things about this team, and the people, which left you with these feelings? (Identify as many as you can.)

How much of this was due to the leadership of the team?

Nine elements for effective teams

There are many elements which contribute towards making effective teams. I have a view that the following nine elements, illustrated in Figure 2.3, cover most of what works.

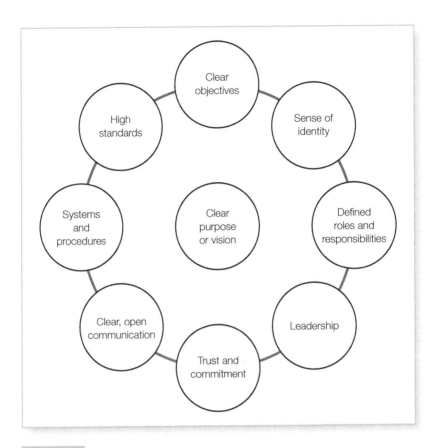

figure 2.3   The nine elements

1   **Clear purpose or vision** – people want to know what they are doing and aiming to achieve and to have something they can commit to. This is something too many team leaders overlook, or they know what their vision is but they forget to share it with the team members. They also overlook the benefits of restating it frequently.

2   **Clear objectives** – there are two parts to this, clear objectives for the team as a whole and for the individual team members so that they know what they need to do and how they will be contributing to the overall performance.

3   **High standards** – effective teams take pride in the performance, the way they work and the level to which they work. Having clear standards of performance or key performance indicators gets a strong commitment – and even more if the team is involved in setting these.

4   **Systems and procedures** – implementing establishing clear ways of working, reporting, interacting and implementing processes can improve efficiency and effectiveness. These can evolve as the team becomes more accustomed to working together and as they recognise the benefits of having them in place.

5   **Clear, open communication** – both formal and informal. Sharing of information, saying what you think and asking for what you want are all essential for effectiveness in a team. It is important that team members listen to each other properly, respecting everyone's contribution or point of view. A part of this is to be comfortable expressing disagreement and dealing with differences – do not duck them – when appropriate!

6   **Trust and commitment** – this is something of an intangible element. Although it can be good if interpersonal relationships are strong, it is not essential in a team. It is more important to be able to respect and work with colleagues, feeling they will do what they promise. Being reliable and trustworthy is far more powerful than liking each other.

7   **Leadership** – as the team develops the style and approach of leadership needs to move with it. The leadership can be shared around the team according to the requirement for different qualities and skills. Wherever it does come from, the team needs leadership whether hands on or hands off.

8   **Defined roles and responsibilities** – most people like to know exactly what they are supposed to do and how they will be assessed against it. It also helps effectiveness within the team because clear definitions can reduce duplication of work and effort and avoid confusion of expectation.

9   **Sense of identity** – do the team members have a sense of belonging? Combining the sense of purpose and vision, a knowledge of your contribution and having clear responsibilities helps everyone feel they are part of something worthwhile. Most human beings like to have a feeling of belonging to something and being valued. Think how many times you see teams and team members create various rituals, tokens, etc. to build this even more.

Using these nine elements assess your team against each of them. (This is very powerful if you get the team to do it from their individual perspectives and then come together to share their thoughts.)

I suggest you rate each element from 0–5 (0 = really poor; 5 = really strong). Combine the scores and from this you can identify the areas for improvement.

Discuss and agree an action plan to improve the identified areas. Remember to set a time frame for each of the steps and how and when you will review them.

Exercise

1 **Clear purpose or vision** – current score: _____
   Actions to improve?

2 **Clear objectives** – current score: _____
   Actions to improve?

3 **High standards** – current score: _____
   Actions to improve?

4 **Systems and procedures** – current score: _____
   Actions to improve?

5 **Clear, open communication** – current score: _____
   Actions to improve?

6 **Trust and commitment** – current score: _____
   Actions to improve?

7 **Leadership** – current score: _____
   Actions to improve?

8 **Defined roles and responsibilities** – current score: _____
   Actions to improve?

9 **Sense of identity** – current score: _____
   Actions to improve?

Summary

- Recognise that all groups and teams move through the four stages from 'forming' through 'storming' on to 'norming' and then 'performing'.

- Although the group progresses through these stages, some individuals may take longer than others to move.

- Think about what the team need from you to help them through the process – and adapt your style and approach.

- What type of team are you leading – work, project, focus or virtual? They will need different things from you and will present you with a variety of challenges.

- Take some time to understand the nine elements of effective teams. Which ones are you more comfortable with and do you feel are more important? (In reality, they are all important, but human nature suggests you will have some preferences – and that's OK!)

- Use the exercise above on the nine elements with your teams. It will really strengthen how well they work and raise their potential for delivering great results.

Reference

[1] Bruce Tuckman, 'Development sequence in small groups', *Psychological Bulletin* 63(6), June 1965.

3

Understanding team roles and balance

When you have to start leading teams, there are a number of factors to consider. Some of them are more obvious than others. One of these is often overlooked, even by more experienced leaders, and that is the need to have a range of roles being covered, which require different skills and characteristics. To help you achieve this we will look at the nature of these roles and how you can identify people's preferences. When you are aware of these roles you can use individuals more effectively by using their preferences and strengths within the team. Getting this balance is a major component of your likely success in teambuilding.

When you need to lead a team to achieve the overall objectives, it is natural to think that you want to create an environment which is positive and in which people feel comfortable working together. This can cause you to pull together a team of similar characters and personalities. Initially, this might make some sense. In reality, it will mean that the team will almost certainly be limited in what they can achieve. Although this is a business book, it might be easier to think about this scenario in some other environments. How good would a concert sound if the orchestra was made up of too many people who were great on strings and could just about make a tune on a brass or woodwind instrument? How many championship sports teams are filled with all-rounders or generalists?

Any successful team will have a combination of different characters. A simple way of splitting them down is to identify the following:

Doers – who are intent on the job that's to be done and give the team its drive and momentum.

Thinkers – who have good ideas and reject bad ones.

Carers – who keep the team together, ease tensions, promote harmony and are sensitive about relationships within the team.

Looking at this in more detail, the reality is that strong, high-performing teams will be built on difference NOT similarity. This is often a challenge for a leader, especially when new to the role. It is also a common error from a number of mediocre or poor managers and leaders. They opt for comfort by filling their team with similar types of people – often cloning themselves where they can. They think that the team will be easier to manage. However, when the team struggles to perform well they become harder to lead and manage!

There are a number of theories or concepts about team roles and team balance. Probably the most widely used is the Belbin®Team Role[1] model, which is used by 40 per cent of the world's top companies in their team working and teambuilding. Although the original work was carried out some years ago it has been worked on and developed since then.

The underlying principle is that balanced teams, able to draw on the range of team roles, will do better than unbalanced teams. Another key finding is that balanced teams will consistently outperform groups of individuals when faced with complex challenges or problems. Although Belbin had a view that a team should be relatively small (four members!), his main message was that a range of specific team roles need to be 'honoured' and the team members can use all of them. Accoring to Belbin, there are nine team roles, or behaviours, which make up the balance for a productive team. As a leader, knowing these nine roles, as well as having an understanding of your own preferred style and those of your team members, means that you can have a significant impact on the way the team performs. It enables you to play to people's strengths which has a double benefit, in terms of both productivity and the individual's motivation. Take it a step further and involve the whole team in raising their awareness and understanding of their own and their colleagues' styles, and the implications for how they can contribute most effectively will help to accelerate the team's effectiveness. It will help to build trust and a greater acceptance of each other and recognition that the differences are good. It will help you to match individuals to specific roles or tasks which will fit with their preferred role, and this will be more positive for all.

The model is not the same as a psychometric profile and the different roles are not meant to be any sort of personality label. They are an indication of a preferred way of working and behaving and most of us can use more than one of the roles. However, there will be some roles that do not suit or fit our own style and it helps to recognise this and avoid these.

The team/task process

When the team has to come together and deliver a result, it will go through a process to achieve this most effectively, as shown in Figure 3.1.

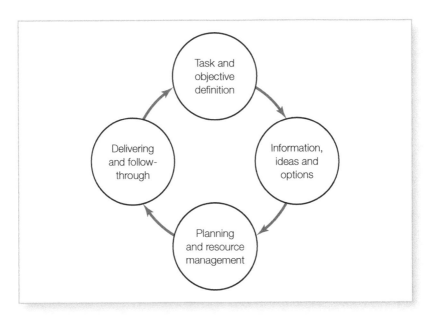

figure 3.1   The team/task process

Each phase will require different skills and qualities and this starts to show why we need a balance of styles and approaches from team members. Some will be good at the planning and organising, others better at the people part of it.

What are the team roles?

The table overleaf gives you an overview of each of the nine roles Belbin identified. They all have certain characteristics which can be an indication of when they are being used by team members. In addition to this, there will be a number of qualities and behaviours which are positive contributions to the team when being used appropriately and constructively. The other side of this is that there will be some potential weaknesses with each role, especially when being used too much.

A key point to emphasise is that there are no better or worse roles within these. The high-performing team needs all of these roles to be covered or attended to at different times. The roles are of equal importance and the balance is the key. Too many team members using just one or two roles, or an absence of some, can cause the team to be inefficient or ineffective.

ROLE	TYPICAL FEATURES	POSITIVE QUALITIES THEY BRING	POTENTIAL WEAKNESSES
PLANT	Individualistic, non-conformist, can be intense. Often happy to work on their own when starting to look at ideas.	Innovative, good thinkers, enjoy challenge of problem solving, brings creative solutions to the team, not limited by current practice and will come up with alternative or new options.	Not always realistic or practical. Puts ideas into the team, but doesn't think through the detail, so can have communication issues. Doesn't handle criticism well, can withdraw if ideas are disregarded or put down.
RESOURCE INVESTIGATOR	Extroverted, enthusiastic, sociable. Good communicator. Stable.	Enjoys being the 'outside' link for the team, dealing with other individuals or groups. Enjoys the challenge of getting hold of information. Likes being out and about and being busy. Builds networks.	Low interest/boredom threshold, often works in bursts. Takes things up and puts them down quickly. Does not always follow through – tends to present the outline and expect others to finish it.
CO-ORDINATOR	Stable, calm, self-assured, disciplined, has natural authority. Natural organiser.	Co-ordinates people and things. Involves others and uses their strengths. Communicates well, likes clear objectives and agendas, will make decisions. Usually well respected.	Not necessarily the brightest ideas person. Can be cautious, more interested in the process than the outcome. Not very competitive.
SHAPER	Energetic, dynamic, goal oriented, determined, overcomes challenges or obstacles, proactive.	Wants things to happen, to achieve goals. Brings energy and drive to the team. Communicative, puts forward suggestions, is ambitious – wants the team to move forward.	Can appear pushy, insensitive to others, single-minded to pursue own aim – not good at considering others' views. Impatient. Not intentionally blunt, but not empathetic to others' views.

Role			
MONITOR/ EVALUATOR	Calm, cautious, serious, logical in approach; can seem negative. The 'devil's advocate' of the team.	Challenges, analyses and evaluates ideas. Judges objectively. Will not support or agree to anything without evaluating it. Prevents team doing anything too rash.	Can seem cold or even negative, always questioning. May appear over-cautious and lack drive. Not always socially skilled, can upset others, e.g. plants.
TEAM WORKER	Social, sensitive, can be quiet, diplomatic, communicator, wants to get on with everyone.	Involves others, communicates freely with team, likes harmony, often good at smoothing friction. Aware of how others are feeling or reacting. Although a 'soft' role, missed when not there.	Dislikes conflict and personal confrontation. Will try to avoid it. Also, can seem indecisive, especially when tough decisions are needed.
IMPLEMENTER	Practical, stable, methodical, disciplined, reliable, conservative.	Takes ideas and converts them into tasks and actions. Conscientious and hard-working. Will adapt and improve, but within a structure and from a basis. Sees things through to a conclusion, completes tasks.	Can be inflexible, not receptive to new ideas or changes of plan. May seem rather staid to some. Somewhat 'status' conscious which can make this person critical of others.
COMPLETER	Conscientious, detail person, perfectionist, can be a worrier. Fussy?	'The dotter of i's and crosser of t's.' Checks and attends to detail. Looks for errors. Concerned with order, will follow through action plans, complete the thoughts of the plant or the shaper.	Unlikely to delegate. 'Only I can do this right.' Can frustrate others, gets bogged down in trivial details.
SPECIALIST	Confident, enjoys acquiring or developing knowledge. Can be quite single-minded and self-starting in this pursuit.	Brings particular technical skill or knowledge to team. Good for specific problems and issues. Keeps learning and developing, so can help to move team's knowledge forward.	Limited contribution if speciality or knowledge not needed. Can be too focused on the technicalities. Not always aware of others, can be intolerant.

Source: Table from Belbin, R. M., *Team Roles at Work* (Butterworth Heinemann, 2nd edn, 2010).

Assessing yourself and your team

You can use various ways to assess your team members and their preferred roles. There are profiles and questionnaires available through Belbin's organisation, which can provide you with an objective view. Alternatively, you can take a more subjective approach, combining observation and discussion. This can still provide you with worthwhile information and has an added benefit of stimulating discussion and involvement with the team members, which can increase their understanding of the concept.

It is rare for anyone to be totally in one of the roles. Most people will have two or three which they can or do use comfortably and naturally. (There may be a strong preference for one of them, but not necessarily.) At the same time, there will be some roles which they would struggle to do and are best avoided. This does leave some in the middle, which could be carried out with the right understanding and guidance.

Start by identifying your own preferred styles. Use the descriptions in the table and work out which you feel are your own 'stronger' team roles. Then consider which you feel do not fit you.

My stronger roles:

My roles to avoid:

Now think about the team members and do the same for them, from your perspective.

When you have done your assessment, it is a good idea to ask the team members to do the exercise for themselves and record their own thoughts.

To really add to the value of this, get the team to share their own assessments and then to have their colleagues give input about their observations of the individual's preferred roles – with reasons for making these. (Do be prepared for some possible disagreements. People's perception of someone may be different from the individual's own self-image. Stress the fact that there are no 'right' or 'ideal' roles.

The key is to raise awareness of how others might see us and to recognise and appreciate the differences. You could expand the discussions to explore why these differences of perception occur.)

Using this exercise helps the team to better understand the benefits of having a balance in the team. They can appreciate the different qualities each role brings to the team and its achievements. The discussion and sharing can be a powerful help for improving understanding of each other, communication and building better working relationships.

Case study

A successful project manager I have known for a number of years uses this exercise frequently. When starting out as a project manager she used to find it a challenge to pull the team together and to become productive quickly. With some of the project deadlines this was a potential problem. After discussing this situation with her, I suggested she used the Belbin tool with any new team, making sure she explained the purpose.

Whenever starting a new project and having to bring together a new team she has a meeting where the focus is on the team roles and team working rather than the project and the outcomes. She briefs the team on the need for balance and the various roles. They work through the steps outlined above. She says this always stimulates a good discussion and leads to an early openness in the way the team interacts.

Once the team members are comfortable with their own preferred team roles (within the project context), it becomes easier to assign responsibilities and actions to the people most suitable for them. This means they can get underway a lot faster because individuals are happier with their role and contribution.

She believes that using this saves several days or even weeks in getting things moving quickly and puts the focus on outputs and achievements rather than getting into debates or arguments about who does what and how. It moves the team from forming through storming a lot more easily too. (Given her current senior position, it would appear to have been effective!)

Checking the team balance

Having discussed the roles and preferences you can capture the team's overall balance using the following table.

List the team members on the left and then indicate the roles:

Exercise

Name / Team role	Plant	Resource investigator	Co-ordinator	Shaper	Monitor evaluator	Team worker	Implementer	Completer	Specialist

Preferred role ✓   Possible role ?   Avoid ✗

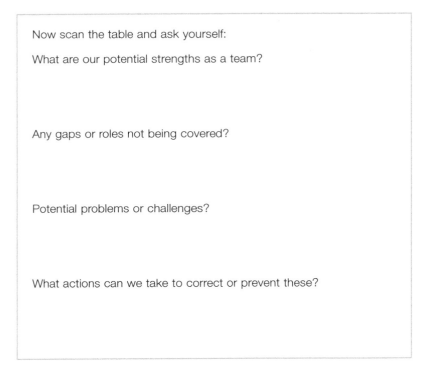

Now scan the table and ask yourself:

What are our potential strengths as a team?

Any gaps or roles not being covered?

Potential problems or challenges?

What actions can we take to correct or prevent these?

Handling the different team roles

One of your challenges when leading a team is to work out how to get the best from individuals so that they can contribute most effectively using their preferred team role. Recognising the differences and being able to adapt your approach is a mark of a good leader. Remember, the tendency for most of us is to aim to influence or interact with others in the way which fits most comfortably with our own style. This is not a criticism, just a statement of fact. However, there is nothing to say you have to follow this path. You can develop greater flexibility by thinking about what you want to do and practising. (And allow yourself not to be perfect straight away.)

The table overleaf gives you some ideas of things to do and things to avoid when influencing people in each of the different team roles.

Team role	Things to do	Things to avoid
Plant	Give them time to explore ideas and allow them to talk.	Forcing them into tight deadlines.
	Listen and be enthusiastic about their ideas.	Rushing them into decisions and action.
	Be tolerant – they may be disorganised and not always punctual! However, when involved with a new project or challenge they bring a lot of energy and ideas.	Being too structured in your approach or expectations of them.
	Give them plenty of positive 'strokes', public recognition and 'pats on the back'.	Imposing rigid structures or timescales that will inhibit their creativity.
	Help them by setting up structures or plans to take their ideas forward. Develop the details of their concept.	Engaging with them without having done some research or checking – the plant can be somewhat arrogant in their attitude.
	Ensure you have some knowledge of the area under discussion, don't pretend!	Using their ideas as if they are your own.
	Focus on the 'How...?' Questions to get conversations flowing. Save the 'What ...?' and 'When...?' until later.	
	Put agreements in writing and keep a record of them.	
Resource investigator	Explore new ideas and possible solutions.	Spending too much time focusing on the past.
	Encourage them to talk and share their thoughts.	Rushing them into a decision – give them time to talk through their ideas.
	Recognise they like to spend time outside the team developing and interacting with their network.	Getting into the details too quickly or for too long.
	Keep things future focused.	Taking issue with their opinions or ideas unless they are way out of line. They will often change them anyway.

Team role	Things to do	Things to avoid
Resource investigator	Make sure they get credit for ideas that are developed.	Getting frustrated by their inability to follow things through or go into the detail behind their ideas or suggestions.
	Keep them on track by using a phrase such as, 'That's a good idea, how do you think we could use it in this situation?'	Going into too much detail when trying to sell them on an idea.
	Look for the ideas you agree with which can help the team and build on them.	
	Accept they will need support and help in taking ideas through in to actions. Whether this means writing up a plan or handing things over to a completer does not matter – just do it!	
	Assure yourself that ideas and plans can be completed in the time available.	
Co-ordinator	Recognise they may have some strong views and beliefs about how things should be.	Curbing or blocking discussion by over stressing your own point or opinion.
	Provide a sense of structure and organisation.	Going off the point or indulging in your own agenda at the expense of the team.
	Keep focus on goals and objectives.	Making them feel undermined by doing 'private deals' or pursuing 'personal conflicts' over their heads or off topic from the agenda.
	Be prepared and organised when meeting with them and at team meetings.	Getting frustrated or impatient with their apparent caution or wish to avoid taking too many risks.
	Offer support and build ideas with them.	
	Be patient, if necessary, as they want to stick to the process or agenda.	

Team role	Things to do	Things to avoid
Co-ordinator	Recognise that this role is not comfortable with too much flexibility.	Being vague or ambiguous in your responses to them – stick to facts.
	Delegate planning and organising meetings or events to them.	
Shaper	Recognise that they will come up with ideas and suggestions for the team (but ones which suit their aims or agenda).	Going off the subject.
	Be business-like in conversations and interactions.	Using 'How...?' questions – they do not want to get involved in the process.
	Use specific questions and statements (e.g. 'What...?') rather than general ones.	
	If you disagree or cannot support their ideas be ready to explain why. Be clear about the reasons.	Bringing in personal issues or attacking them personally.
	Make sure you, or someone, deals with the detail of any task or idea – shapers will be on to the next goal!	Promising to follow something through or to handle the details and then not doing so.
	Acknowledge their contribution and ideas.	
	Be prepared to give the shaper feedback if they are being over-pushy and upsetting other team members. (They are not usually too sensitive to others' feelings or responses.)	
Monitor evaluator	Use their strengths as a practical, careful and analytical team member.	Surprising them with requests.
	Be patient with them.	Rushing them for an opinion or decision.
	Let them have information or outlines of plans before meetings.	Just focusing on the future and not reflecting on the past.
	Be ready to discuss details.	Over-selling new ideas or plans.
	Give them time to question or challenge. Also, they may take time to explain their point of view. Show understanding.	Being over-enthusiastic or optimistic. Using arguments based on subjective ideas rather than facts or solid information.
	Explain things in a well thought out and structured way.	Dropping in unexpectedly with new ideas or proposals.

Team role	Things to do	Things to avoid
Monitor evaluator	Point out disadvantages as well as advantages in any plans. Give them time to consider issues especially if proposing new ways of doing things.	Presenting ideas without thinking them through – you may find yourself exposed on any subsequent discussions. Imposing unproven ideas.
Implementer	Be thoroughly prepared when explaining plans or goals for the team or for them. Either have a procedure for how you want things done or involve them in creating one. Allow them to take ideas and work out how to implement them. They are good at finding and following practical ways of doing things. Speak clearly, logically and precisely.	Giving opinions and options – stick to facts and keep things practical. Wasting time – implementers want to be doing! Being ambiguous – be clear about what you want or expect.
	Allow them space and time to think things through. They are more likely to be good listeners rather than speakers. Give clear explanations of what you want or expect – and why.	
Team worker	Recognise their contribution in helping the overall harmony and communication in the team. Show understanding of their values and beliefs. Allow them time to share interests and aspirations. Encourage plenty of communication from them when they appear to want to join in. Be general with you questions, e.g. 'How do you feel about the situation?' Wait for their answer and show you understand their feelings.	Forcing them to speak up or contribute. Ignoring their feelings, values and beliefs. Getting impatient or pushy with them and not allowing them time or space to express themselves. Pressing them into leading the team or making tough decisions.

Team role	Things to do	Things to avoid
Completer	Be practical and factual when explaining things. Show how they relate to current practices.	Making last-minute changes or plans.
	Explain things in steps, making the process clear.	Being vague or too general in discussions or with plans. Be specific and show they are thought through.
	Give notice about possible changes.	Making changes without taking time to explain the reasons.
	Stick to what you discuss or promise.	Giving tasks and deadlines without thinking them through.
	Help them to avoid becoming frustrated with plants and resource investigators.	
	Recognise their contribution in paying attention to detail and challenging things which are not thought through.	
Specialist	Recognise and value their technical or specialist knowledge.	Under-valuing their specialist contribution.
	Give them the opportunity to speak from their experience.	Involving them too much in their non-specialist areas.
	Accept they may tune out when discussions are away from their area of expertise.	Ignoring them. They may still have something valuable to contribute to the team even if it is outside of their expertise.
	Make them feel they've been brought in especially to help.	Criticising or under-estimating their profession or expertise.
	Keep within their sphere of knowledge or specialism.	
	Encourage them to share ideas and involve others – and to delegate where they can.	

Making the most of your team

Working your way through this chapter might make you feel as though leading a team is highly complex and challenging. In many ways it is. People (your team members) will provide a challenge because they bring their different characters and personalities to work, combined with so many other variables which affect their mood of the day. They will be positive and fired up some days, neutral and just do their jobs on others, and feel fed up, demotivated or negative on others. As a leader you have to deal with them across all of these attitudes and moods. One way to get the team to engage with you and follow you more readily is to be able to treat them in the right way – by playing to their strengths and using the qualities they bring. It is worth spending some time rereading this chapter to fully understand the principles.

Summary

- Identify who are the 'doers', 'thinkers' and 'carers' in your team. How do they act when together? What qualities do you feel they bring to the team?
- Read through and understand the different team roles in the Belbin model. Which are your natural or preferred roles? Which do you think are those best avoided for you?
- Think of some specific examples of how you have used your preferred roles when working in teams.
- Consider each of your team members and work out what you feel are their preferred roles. Identify the specific behaviours they use in the team which makes you think that these are their preferences.
- Involve the team in understanding the concept and identifying their own roles. From here assess how the team is balanced using the table on pages 32–33. Agree how you can avoid any problems from too many similar roles or handle where there might be gaps.
- Make time to practise the 'do' and 'things to avoid' behaviours to influence the team members according to their preferred roles.

Reference

[1] Dr Meredith Belbin, *Team Roles at Work*, Butterworth Heinemann, 2nd edn, 2010.

4

Your role as a leader

You will become clearer about the principles of leadership in this chapter. I will help you to understand the difference between leadership and management and the implications for your own role. You will be introduced to the fundamental elements of both Action Centred Leadership and Situational Leadership® and how you can apply each of them to your teams. As you develop your understanding of these you will recognise the benefits of becoming more flexible in your leadership approach, to adapt to the needs of the individuals and the team.

A challenge for many of you reading this is understanding exactly what leadership is and what your role is as a leader. To complicate this further, your bosses might have their own expectation which could be different from yours. As we saw in Chapter 1, many people are promoted because they are good at 'doing' their previous job and are moved up with little or no help or development for the new responsibilities of the management role. Therefore, feeling comfortable moving into the leadership part of the role takes time.

Many organisations are quite efficient at sorting out their management processes and systems. Those in the management positions are comfortable working with these for a variety of reasons. However, as Warren Bennis observed in *On Becoming a Leader*, 'Failing organisations are usually over-managed and under-led.'[1]

Directing and leading an organisation is different from managing one. This is very true when considering teams. People want leaders and leadership rather than managing. The number of definitions of leadership run into the hundreds, with thousands of books available on the subject. So, what is leadership? What is the difference between management and leadership?

Management ('Managers do things right')

Management is about getting things done. It requires co-ordination of resources to achieve a defined end result (objective or target) with and through people. It is the science of continuous improvement.

Leadership ('Leaders do the right things')

Leadership is the development of a vision and direction, setting a course that gives a sense of common purpose. Leadership is about inspiring, involving, persuading and motivating people to follow the cause and achieve the vision. Leadership is innovating and initiates change. Leadership is being able to get people to follow you.

Put more simply, management is about processes and tasks. Leadership is mostly about behaviour and people. The two are not mutually exclusive. Management without leadership is possible and can achieve business results, although it will be harder work because people may not be engaged or motivated. Leadership without management is also likely to be less than fully effective because the control and monitoring may not happen. Bringing the two together is the way forward.

When looking at leadership there are three levels: team, operational and strategic (see Figure 4.1). Although there are a number of similarities in the qualities and requirements across all three levels, there are differences too. Senior managers and leaders in an organisation need to provide the medium- and long-term vision. Their leadership style and approach needs to keep people focused on that horizon and make sure that the organisation is set up to work towards it. The other leaders, from middle management through to team leaders, are more functional. They need to provide the vision, direction and plan to achieve more specific tasks or activities in a shorter or even immediate timescale.

figure 4.1   Levels of leadership

Think about your own experiences so far, both at work and outside.

Who are the people you think of who were good leaders in your experience?

What, specifically, did they do in the way they behaved and acted which makes you think of them so positively?

You may have had to struggle to choose many good leaders from your past. Unfortunately, many of our experiences are towards the other end of the scale and exposed us to people who were either not very good or even poor leaders. This may not be their fault. They may have had no training or guidance on how they are supposed to behave. Not all leaders are born to the role! In fact, most are not and, fortunately, leadership is something which can be learned and developed. The key for good leadership is being someone that people are willing to follow.

To achieve this it helps if you have some, or all, of these qualities of a good leader:

Integrity – being open and truthful (as far as you can). Essential to generate trust in the team.

Positive – a belief in what is possible, focusing on what can be achieved, projecting the right level of enthusiasm.

Determined – willing to persevere through challenging times, to overcome setbacks.

Sincere – linked with integrity, being true and not creating false hope or making rash promises.

Sensitive – having an awareness of the team members, what is happening for them, when to offer support, when to push.

Toughness – setting and following through on high standards, expecting people to perform, at the same time being consistent and fair, making decisions.

Humility – open to learning, asking for others' ideas and input, giving credit to others.

Warmth – interested in others, being approachable.

Communication – sharing information, providing the vision, listening, listening, listening.

Developer – bringing out the best in others, delegating, coaching, training.

You may have some additional qualities which you feel are important for a good leader. Feel free to add them. How would you rate yourself against each of the qualities? How do you think your team members would rate you?

When looking at your leadership with your team, it can be useful to understand two different approaches. Each of them can offer you some insights that can help you, depending on the circumstances or the individuals you are leading. You can choose to use either, or even both, depending on the circumstances.

Functional leadership

The principle here is that the effective leader will see that a number of functions are completed, and by keeping these in mind the task will be accomplished and the team will be involved in doing it. Professor John Adair (Sandhurst and University of Surrey) developed his model called Action Centred Leadership[2, 3] to help to develop leaders using the functional approach. This is extremely useful to understand and apply when addressing specific tasks and leading project teams.

When at Sandhurst, he identified that the more successful leaders paid attention to three areas, as shown in Figure 4.2.

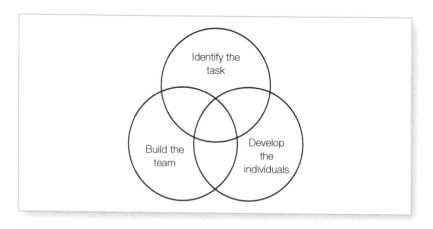

figure 4.2   **Action-centred leadership**
Figure from Adair, J., *Action-Centred Leadership* (Gower Publishing Ltd, 1979)

Many leaders, and especially new or inexperienced ones, find that they are more comfortable in one or two of these areas, spending more time and energy in these at the expense of the other. This is natural, but it does have an impact on the effectiveness of their leadership.

Does this ring any bells for you? As you look at the table overleaf, can you identify any areas where you prefer to spend your time? Others which make you less comfortable?

Adair identified what the leader needs to do within each of these areas in order to achieve the task. He also created a list of the main functions the leader should keep in mind. Action in any one of these will impact on each of the three circles in Figure 4.2.

1 **Defining the task**: This sets a clear objective for the team. The team and the individuals need to have a collective goal to aim for. If the leader does not seem to have a clear objective or vision, it would appear they do not know where they want to go. If they do not know, why should the team follow them?

2 **Planning**: Both leader and team need to be aware of timescales, resources required and available, constraints and responsibilities to achieve efficiency and clarity of working together.

3 **Briefing**: This involves giving and receiving information and summarising ideas. Keeping the team and individuals involved by sharing information and getting their input encourages a sense of inclusion.

4 **Controlling**: The leader needs to implement effective control systems on the group and individuals. This ensures standards are met to achieve the task and builds confidence in your leadership capabilities from individuals and teams.

5 **Evaluating**: Continual evaluation of individual and group performance against the plan is essential for developing and maintaining standards and skills. Any variance needs to be spotted quickly and action taken to get back on track.

6 **Motivating**: Paying attention to how people are performing and interacting is key for a leader. Good communication, setting goals and providing feedback are just some of the things which help this. Also, being alert to signs of demotivation – and taking action to remove them – is essential.

7 **Organising**: Efficient allocation of all the resources, including people, makes the task more achievable and supports motivation for individuals and teams by providing a clear action plan.

8 **Providing examples**: Leading by example builds credibility with teams and individuals and helps build motivation and efficiency in individuals. Being a good role model is often underestimated as a leadership quality. Remember, when you are in a leadership position *people pay more attention to what you do, not what you say*!

Things to consider when applying Action Centred Leadership

The table below gives you some pointers to help you when using Action Centred Leadership with your team. For each of the three 'circle' areas we suggest the goals you may have. This is followed by some ideas for how you can achieve these goals. You may find it helpful to make a copy of this and the next table (the prompt for Action Centred Leadership) and use them as a checklist.

Task	Team	Individual
Leaders' goals		
1 Achieving the best result or outcome.	1 Ensuring individuals work as a team.	1 Meeting individuals' needs/goals.
2 Ensuring that the team and individuals accomplish their goals in most effective way.	2 Containing unproductive and negative conflict.	2 Avoiding frustrations and demotivation.
	3 Managing tensions within the team so that it does not disintegrate.	3 Maintaining individuals' involvement and preventing withdrawal.
	4 Move through towards 'norming' and 'performing'.	4 Creating satisfaction with the activity and its outcome.
How to achieve the goals		
▪ Be clear about the task and its measure and any restraints.	▪ Brief the team fully and regularly.	▪ Ensure everyone is clear about their role.
▪ Be aware of available resources and organise them.	▪ Consult the team before making major decisions which affect them.	▪ Establish clear standards.
▪ Plan the way forward and identify the mileposts.	▪ Develop team spirit and support.	▪ Recognise and encourage skills and abilities.
▪ Monitor progress and evaluate results.	▪ Maintain discipline and control using agreed standards.	▪ Give the right amount of responsibility and challenge.
▪ Identify gaps or under-performance and remedy quickly, e.g. more resources, coaching/training.	▪ Communicate progress and success as often as possible.	▪ Give regular feedback so they know how they are doing.
		▪ Provide coaching or help to raise standard if needed.

Prompt for using Action Centred Leadership

KEY FUNCTIONS	TASK	TEAM	INDIVIDUAL
DEFINE OBJECTIVES	Identify task and constraints	Involve team Share commitment	Clarify aims Gain acceptance
PLAN/ ORGANISE	Establish priorities Check resources and constraints Decide and action plan	Consult and involve Agree standards Structure and roles	Assess skills and capabilities Set targets Delegate
INFORM/ CONFIRM	Brief group and check understanding	Answer questions Obtain feedback Encourage ideas/ actions	Advise Listen Enthuse and inspire
SUPPORT/ MONITOR	Report progress Maintain standards Discipline and control	Co-ordinate Reconcile conflict Develop suggestions	Assist/reassure Recognise effort Counsel if struggling
EVALUATE	Summarise progress Review objectives Adjust plan if necessary	Recognise success Learn from failure	Assess performance Appraise Guide and train

Source: Table from Adair, J., *Action-Centred Leadership* (Gower Publishing Ltd, 1979)

Case study

A young manager, Adam, was struggling to engage his team to commit to projects and other day-to-day assignments. He had joined the retail marketing team in a bank from a competitor and was highly competent and capable in his role and he brought a lot of enthusiasm and new ideas to the department. However, he was taking over from a manager who was somewhat demotivated and this had spread to the team members. Just to add to the challenge of the role, many of the team were older and some had thought they should have been offered the role.

▶

In his previous company, Adam had only had a small team of four people to lead. Now he had ten with two supervisors. He thought he was an open, supportive manager who communicated well. However, he was finding it tough to engage the team and they would find plenty of reasons why they could not commit to new challenges or projects. It was getting to the point where Adam was under pressure from his bosses to get the team working better and he was feeling rather disillusioned and demotivated, and his confidence was getting lower by the day.

Luckily, the bank had organised some teambuilding and leadership training for many of its managers. One of the ideas covered was using Action Centred Leadership and it provided a framework for reviewing many of the activities during the training. Following the workshop, Adam decided to take time to think how he could use the principles of addressing the needs of the three circles in a balanced way and working through the functions. He realised that one of the things he needed to do was to engage with people on an individual level before briefing the team. This was important because it meant he could get a number of the team to be more supportive and committed first and they would be more positive in the group briefing.

The first new task he approached this way proved to be more successful. Not perfectly smooth and easy, but noticeably better. With determination and perseverance the next couple were even more positive in both what was achieved and how. The overall department performance was improving and morale and commitment were stronger. Having said that, two of the more negative team members left, with some encouragement as they would not work to the newly agreed standards.

Adam's review with his boss was positive, the feedback from the team members was supportive and the internal customers within the bank were more than happy with the service and initiatives coming from his department. Something has been working well: three years on and Adam has been promoted twice and gets his supervisors to use the checklists he developed to lead their teams.

Situational Leadership®

There are many models which look at leadership from a behavioural point of view. The 'how' of leadership rather than the 'what' of the functional leadership approach. At the root of many of the behavioural models is the balance between the leader's concern for results or achieving goals and their concern for the people or relationship. As you can see from Figure 4.3, this gives the leader a choice of four fundamental styles they can use. When you look at these options there is one which looks as though it would be most people's preference, the high task, high relationship quadrant. (The task axis is talking about the degree of direction and instruction the leader gives about what the task is, how it needs to be done, timescales, etc. The relationship axis is looking at the personal interaction and how much dialogue is involved. It is *not* about how approachable the leader is or whether they like the team member.) There are two options which you might be comfortable with some of the time, but who would want to admit to being in the low task, low relationship area?

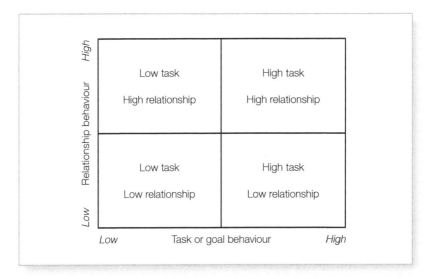

figure 4.3   The style of the leader

This approach of looking at the leader's basic style started a lot of discussion on many training programmes. Could people change their natural or preferred style? If you were already in high task, high relationship, why do you need to do anything else? However, some academics in the USA, notably in California, started to suggest that maybe this was putting the attention on the wrong thing. Rather than worrying about the leader and their style, shouldn't the focus be put on to the followers and what would work best for them? If you have five people in your team, why would one style be right for all of them all of the time? You are dealing with five different personalities, who probably have different skills or capability levels for each of their key tasks, and also bring different attitudes to these tasks. With all of these variables, one style is only likely to hit the spot some of the time. The skilful leader recognises they need to be flexible to adapt to suit the individual and the situation.

The work originally done by Hersey[4] and Blanchard[5] when working at UCLA suggested looking at the 'followers' and assessing them before deciding on the most effective style to use. I like the original definitions where they talked about the followers' 'maturity' level. This can be considered in two areas: their 'task maturity' which refers to the skill and capability level for the specific task; and their 'willingness maturity' which is their attitude and approach to the task. The other factor to consider when looking at Situational Leadership and the follower is that it is task specific. There are some areas of our work that we are skilled at and enjoy doing; others where we struggle with the task but are enthusiastic and want to do it better; and others where we have the skills but dislike doing it and have to be pushed into it. All combinations are possible!

The maturity levels were broken down into four groups:

M1 – People at this level lack the knowledge, skills or confidence to work on their own, and they often need to be pushed to take the task on.

M2 – At this level, followers might be willing to work on the task, but they still don't have the skills to do it successfully without some support or guidance.

M3 – Here, followers are ready and willing to help with the task. They have demonstrated their capability with the task, but they still might not be fully confident in their abilities.

M4 – These followers are able to work on their own and have shown this and enjoy some degree of independence. They have high confidence and strong skills and are committed to the task.

How do you adapt your style to be more effective? Figure 4.4 shows you how to aim for the best fit. You can see how the maturity scale for the followers runs across. You work out where the follower is for the specific task and look straight up and see where you meet the curve.

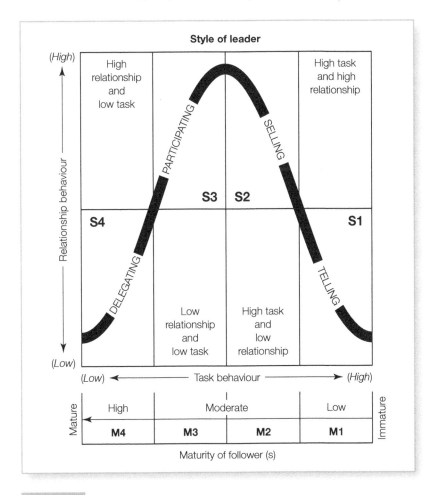

figure 4.4 **Situational Leadership**

For someone at M1 use the S1 style – telling or directing. You give clear instructions and guidelines, with very little two-way communication and very few questions.

Moving to M2 use S2 – selling or coaching. You are still giving guidance and setting the direction. This time there is more discussion and interaction, questions and explanation.

M3 requires you to use S3 – participating or joining. This step is often a challenge for many leaders. The biggest shift here is that you are doing less directing and letting go of some of the control. You want more input and ideas from the follower and are open to considering their suggestions.

M4 goes to S4 – delegating. Allowing the follower freedom to get on with the task, with little discussion about the detail or the way they will do it. The leader will still monitor without interfering.

Although you will have a preferred 'natural' style, probably with another you use some of the time, to be a really effective leader you need to develop the flexibility to move across all four of the styles. The key to effective leadership is to find the right style for each follower and the task – adapting to the situation.

Situational Leadership is particularly useful when dealing with individual team members because it encourages you to adapt and choose the most effective approach. It can also be applied in team or group settings. As the team moves through the stages of group development, you might find that the four styles within Situational Leadership will fit. They may not be an exact best fit, but as a starting point it can help you move the team forward.

Forming ⇨ S1 Telling or directing

Storming ⇨ S2 Selling or coaching

Norming ⇨ Participating or joining

Performing ⇨ Delegating or monitoring

Applying leadership with your team

" The task of the leader is to get his or her people from where they are to where they have never been.

Henry Kissinger

The good thing with both Action Centred and Situational Leadership is that each is strong and useful on its own. What is even better is that they are not mutually exclusive and there are times when you can combine them and be even more effective as a leader.

To start to develop your leadership skills you need to become comfortable with the idea of being a leader. (You can help yourself with this by looking for opportunities to lead, possibly outside the workplace. Practice helps whatever the context.)

Take time to understand and assess your people – your team members. What are their skill levels, their strengths and weaknesses? What attitudes do they bring to their roles and to the team? This is necessary for both of the leadership models.

The only leadership style that matters is the one which each team member feels you use – the one they perceive.

Consider using a checklist for each of the main functions of a leader. In it, cover what you need to do for the team and for individuals.

Much is said about the need to plan work, plan resources, etc. If you accept that people are your main resource – *take time to plan your people!*

Remember, you *earn* respect – the best way to *get* respect is to *give* respect.

Summary

- Accept that leadership is an imprecise science.
- Some people seem to be natural leaders; however, nearly everyone can be a leader, or a better leader, if they work at it.
- People look to their leaders to provide a sense of direction or purpose, structure for how the team will work together, support for their on-going efforts and to communicate how things are going.
- We judge our leaders by what they do and how they do it. Check the qualities of a good leader and see how you would rate on each. Where could you improve and how?
- Look at the functions a leader needs to address and think how comfortable you are with each. How do you feel about handling these with each of the three circles? (Many of us are less comfortable with one or two of these – think about how you can become more at ease with them.)
- Understand your team members' 'maturity' levels for specific tasks.
- Practise using each of the four styles within the Situational Leadership model. You will find one or two you are comfortable with as they are your natural style. The others will be something of a stretch! Stick with it because you need to be able to use whichever is the most suitable to be the most effective leader.
- Recognise that your leadership development is a lifelong process.

Key roles of an effective team leader

- Provide the vision and direction
- Clarify roles and responsibilities
- Set clear objectives and standards
- Establish shared ownership
- Communicate clearly and frequently and openly
- Develop the potential of the team members
- Monitor progress and performance
- Encourage group involvement and decisions
- Walk the talk – be a good role model
- Stretch the team, individually and collectively

References

[1] Warren Bennis, *On Becoming a Leader*, Perseus Publishing, 1994.

[2] John Adair, *Action-Centred Leadership*, McGraw-Hill, 1973.

[3] John Adair, *Effective Leadership*, PanMacmillan, 1988 (1983).

[4] Dr Paul Hersey, *The Situational Leader*, Pfeiffer & Co., 1992.

[5] Kenneth Blanchard, Patricia Zigarmi and Dean Zigarmi, *Leadership and The One Minute Manager*, Jossey Bass, 1996.

part

Doing it

5

Setting the direction for your team

> If you don't know where you're going, any road will get you there.
>
> *Lewis Carroll,* Alice in Wonderland

One of the most critical tasks for a leader is to set the direction. If you do not provide a sense of where you want the team to go, why should they follow you? This needs to be done for the team and the individual members of that team. Following on from the previous chapter, the setting of goals or objectives is vital across each of the three circles of the Action Centred Leadership model. We will show you a number of ways of doing this which will give you some options to choose from to suit the individuals and the specific objectives. Additionally, we will consider what else you can do to increase the probability of the objectives being achieved.

When setting the direction for your team it will help if a number of elements are in place, as shown in Figure 5.1 (overleaf). The ultimate direction indicator should come from the *vision* of the organisation. If you are responsible for running an organisation you should ensure that you have a clear vision so that both your clients and the market know what you are aiming to do or to be. It also provides a clear message to all internal personnel about the overall direction. In many cases this vision provides the basis for departments or teams to define their vision.

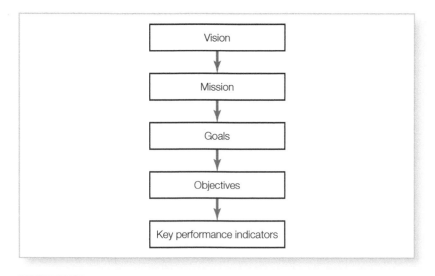

figure 5.1   Setting the direction

Creating vision statements is not as straightforward as it may appear. Being able to develop a clear vision which gives the direction while being succinct takes time and work. The vision statement gives a general sense of direction while being cleverly vague. If it is well done it does not need to be changed unless there is a significant shift in strategy. Some of these examples might help to illustrate what makes a good vision statement:

> *Our Vision is to put joy in kids' hearts and a smile on parents' faces.*
>
> Toys R Us

> *To organize the world's information and make it universally accessible and useful.*
>
> Google

> *To be the company that best understands and satisfies the product, service and self-fulfilment needs of women – globally.*
>
> Avon

> *To provide branded products and services of superior quality and value that improve the lives of the world's consumers.*
>
> Proctor & Gamble

> *To become the most successful premium manufacturer in the car industry.*
>
> BMW

> *To be earth's most customer centric company; to build a place where people can come to find and discover anything they might want to buy online.*
>
> Amazon

To make people happy.

Disney

The vision is stating where you want to be. The mission statement puts more emphasis on the 'what' and 'how'. The mission statement is aimed internally to let people know how their day-to-day work is contributing towards the vision.

As a leader this flow from the vision down, as shown in Figure 5.1, applies to working with your team, regardless of its function or level within the organisation. If there is a vision for your organisation, use that as a starting point, and whatever your team is tasked to achieve think about how it fits with this. You now have something to use to begin to develop your vision. There is not the same need or pressure to make your vision as 'clever' as the organisation's. You want to have something you can express to your team and which they can understand and tell to others if and when required. (When this is in place you can move on, although with your team the need for a mission statement is not required unless you feel like creating one.)

The next steps often cause managers and leaders some problems, differentiating between goals and objectives. Very often these are considered to be interchangeable and that it does not really matter which you use. To some extent that is true, but there is value in understanding the difference and sticking to it. Both will contribute to providing the direction, they just do it at different levels and degree of detail.

Goals v objectives

	Goals	Objectives
Level	Broad plan and scope	Specific plan and narrow scope
Style	Intangible, hard to measure	Tangible, can be measured
Timescale	Longer term	Short to medium term
Content	Ideas and emotions	Facts and details
Intention	Aspirational	Action oriented
Detail	Larger in size and scale	Manageable chunks
Language	Expressed more subjectively	Expressed with actions and outcomes

Goals are often expressed more emotionally and appear to be softer because they do not have to be specific. Objectives will use language which is more detailed and specific and non-emotional. The objectives will be part of the process of achieving the goals or at least moving in that direction. They contain a greater degree of commitment.

Examples of goals and objectives:

Goals:

We will be the best project team in the organisation.

We will be the most successful product development group the company has had.

Objectives:

We will complete 95 per cent of projects ahead of schedule and within budget in this financial year.

We will develop XX new products to go to market in the next year.

Using these examples, you can see the difference between the two. It is possible to recognise whether or not you have achieved objectives.

Think about the team you are leading at the moment, or one you might need to lead in the near future, and work through this exercise. You can tackle this on your own or wait until you are with your team members and involve them. Another option is to develop your own thoughts and then involve the team members and get their input, and decide whether to refine or change anything.

Exercise

Vision statement: What do you want the team to be seen as or to be able to do and deliver?

Can you create a one- or two-sentence description for this?

Goals: Identify one to three goals for the team, remembering that they will be more medium to long term and can be imprecise and subjective.

1

2

3

The power of objectives

These days it is common in an individual's appraisal to use company-wide objectives as a basis for cascading down to specific ones for the people. When it was first introduced back in the 1950s by Peter Drucker in *The Practice of Management*, management by objectives (MBO) challenged the way many organisations and leaders operated.[1] The concept was that the top level leaders made sure that they had clear objectives for each of eight key areas:

Area	Examples
Marketing	Market share, customer satisfaction, product range, sales
Innovation	R&D, new products launched, better processes, using technology
Productivity	Optimum use of resources, focus on core activities, outputs
Physical and financial resources	Business locations, finance, supplies, financial management
Profitability	Profit, margins, rates of return on investment
Management	Management structure, promotion and development of people
Employees	Organisational structure, employee relations, staff retention
Public responsibility	Legal compliance, social and ethical behaviour, corporate social responsibility

Once the objectives are known at the top level, the principle of MBO is that there is a participative process for cascading these down through the organisation, so that each person has their own clearly stated and defined objectives and standards. The thinking is that when employees are involved with the goal setting and choosing of action plans they are more committed and likely to achieve the desired results. The process has all levels jointly identifying their common objectives, defining areas of responsibility and the expected results for each individual. This enables the organisation and its leaders to assess everyone's contribution. As Figure 5.2 (overleaf) shows, the cascade can work all the way from the top, through the team objectives to each team member.

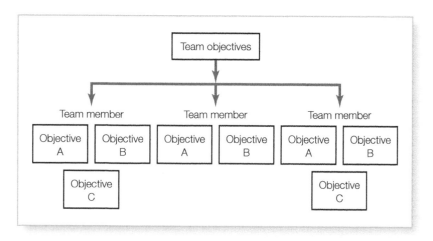

figure 5.2   Cascading objectives

> ❝ Management by objective works – if you know the objectives. Ninety percent of the time you don't.
>
> *Peter Drucker, 1954*

According to one study, where there is a strong commitment to the MBO process from the CEO there was a 56 per cent improvement in productivity and there were also improvements across many other areas of business performance. Where there was minimal commitment from above, the figure was only 6 per cent.[2]

One of the significant benefits of MBO is that it makes sure that the organisation's objectives are shared throughout the workforce. This increases the likelihood of people understanding the objectives and their contribution towards achieving them. More recently, as the popularity of MBO has diminished, it seems that this understanding has reduced. 'A mere 7 per cent of employees today fully understand their company's business strategies and what's expected of them in order to help achieve company objectives.'[3] This is a shame, because a recent study showed that in strong performing companies, 44 per cent of personnel had complete objective alignment from senior management down through the company.[4] When asked, the companies which were weak performers in business terms, 0 per cent of them were aligned with the overall objectives and people did not understand the connection between their role and the company's objectives.

Many theories of motivation feature the power of the feeling we get when we achieve something. This was researched as far back as the late 1960s in the work of Dr Edwin Locke. In his 1968 article 'Toward a Theory of Task Motivation and Incentives', he made the point that employees were motivated by clear objectives and appropriate recognition and feedback.[5] He went on to say that working towards an objective provided a major source of motivation to actually reach it – which, in turn, improved performance.

Apart from contributing to motivation, Locke's research showed that there is a relationship between the difficulty of the objective and how specific it is and people's performance of a task. He found that specific and challenging objectives led to better task performance than vague or easy ones. People get more satisfaction from achieving a stretching objective than from an easy one requiring little effort.

Dr Gary Latham also looked at the impact of objectives in the workplace a few years later. His results supported exactly what Locke had found, that there was a link between objective setting and performance.[6] They then worked together and in 1990 published *A Theory of Objective Setting and Task Performance*. In this book, they reinforced the need to set specific and difficult objectives, and they outlined three other characteristics of successful objective setting (see 1–3 in the list below).

Five principles of objective setting

To motivate, objectives must:

1 have clarity
2 challenge
3 have commitment
4 have feedback
5 have task complexity

Clarity

Effective objectives will be clear, specific and unambiguous. Everyone knows what is expected, and the leader can use the specific outcome as a source of motivation. When an objective is vague it has limited motivational value. To improve your team's performance, set clear objectives that use specific and measurable standards. 'Reduce job turnover by 15 per cent' or 'Respond to customer enquiries within 24 hours' are examples of clear objectives. (You will see how this can be achieved when using the SMARTER process in the next section.)

Challenge

One of the most important elements of effective objectives is having the right level of challenge. People are motivated by achievement, and they will judge how well they have done with an objective based on their anticipated degree of accomplishment. However, be careful not to make objectives too stretching so that they are not achieved because that can be demotivating.

When setting objectives, make each a challenge. If an objective is too easy and not viewed as very important – and if you or your team member does not expect the outcome to be significant – then the effort may not be impressive. Also, the amount of motivation may be minimal or non-existent. Getting the balance right is a challenge in itself.

Commitment

Whether individual or team objectives, it is essential that they are understood and people buy into them. This can be achieved by involving them in the setting of the objectives, although this is not essential. People need to understand how their objectives fit into the organisation's plans and their own role. If you are able to encourage your team to share in the objective setting and tell them how these fit with the vision, they are more likely to be committed to achieving the desired results.

Feedback

Most of us like to know how we are doing against what is expected. This feedback can take many forms, including being able to work it out for ourselves. Having clearly defined standards, expectations and milestones will allow the leader to give regular and more spontaneous feedback while the team member can also assess their own performance.

One of your challenges as a leader is to identify which of your team members need and value 'external' feedback from you and other sources and which are more comfortable in a more 'internal' mode and self-managing. Getting these the wrong way round can lead to some level of demotivation. The 'external' people will often give you clues because they will ask how they are doing or keep seeking approval and reassurance, whereas the 'internal' ones will get on doing their own thing and may seem to ignore or discount any feedback you give. Another thing to be aware of with 'externals' is that they may take feedback to heart and over-react to any critical messages.

Task complexity

When setting objectives that are complex, care needs to be taken that they do not appear too overwhelming. As a leader you need to be aware of the potential for this to happen and also to know which individuals might take on too much if not kept in check (without restricting their motivation and enthusiasm). Make sure that the objective is broken into the right sized chunks to allow for the complexity of the task and allow sufficient time for each of these and the overall objective. You need to maximise the probability of success.

Setting objectives

Be 'SMARTER'

You may be familiar with the SMART model when setting objectives. It has been around for many years and is widely used in many organisations and within most functions. The term was invented by G.T. Doran way back in 1981.[7] We will look at this model in some detail, but it is not always the most effective method. Many organisations have instead adopted SMARTER (as opposed to SMART) as their objective setting approach, because the additional two letters are a good reminder for managers to stay on top of the process. There are some other methods for setting objectives, and we will cover two more in this section. A point to stress here is that they are not mutually exclusive and can be combined. The important thing is to find a method which works for the team and for individuals and helps them to achieve the desired outcome.

Let us start with SMARTER and the steps to take to make it more than a token exercise.

S for SPECIFIC (which is where many go wrong from the start and make things too vague)

This step should make things explicit so that there is no room for misinterpretation.

The following questions can help to keep this step specific:

- What needs to be done? (Express this as a positive, e.g. 'We will build . . . ', 'I will save . . . ' and don't use negative phrases, 'We will stop . . . ', 'I want to give up . . . ') Aim to use action verbs where you can.
- What will be the outcome or result?

- Why is this important?
- Who is responsible? Who else needs to be involved?
- What requirements/constraints are involved?

M for MEASURABLE

Many objectives are easy to measure because they are quantifiable and use numbers or percentages or produce a finite outcome. We can track these results easily. The challenge is for the more qualitative objectives where the outcome might be more subjective. With these you need to be able to define the behavioural criteria or evidence which will indicate that the outcome is what is wanted. (Although not true every time, if you cannot answer the question, 'How will you, or others, know you have achieved XXXX?' it is probably not specific enough.)

It is useful to remember the saying from the early days of MBO, 'If you can't measure it, you can't manage it.' Also, if it cannot be measured, how do you, or anyone, know if the objective is achieved? If this is the case, how can someone feel motivated?

A for ACHIEVABLE (or sometimes for AGREED)

As mentioned in the previous section, setting the objectives at the right level is a key element. They need to be stretching and ambitious but not so much that they are unachievable. At the same time, making objectives too easy will not be motivating.

These questions can help with this step:

- Is this objective within my control?
- Can I/we get it done in the proposed time frame?
- Do I understand the limitations and constraints?
- Can we do this with the resources we have?
- Is this possible and practical?

R for RELEVANT (or sometimes, if linked with AGREED, it is REALISTIC, which is similar to ACHIEVABLE)

Individuals and the team need to see how the objective is relevant to their role and the overall direction of the team. This enables people to see how their work is contributing to the overall organisation objectives. Another aspect of being relevant is to ensure that the different objectives are supporting each other and not creating any conflict or tensions.

T for TIME-BOUND

Most of us work better to deadlines. This step is about setting the *deadline* for the achievement of the objective. It creates a sense of urgency. Without a set deadline, you will reduce the motivation and urgency required to execute tasks for many people. Deadlines create the focus and help to set priority and prompt action.

There is one simple question:

▪ When will this objective be completed?

E is EVALUATED

Once the objective is set, it is important (or even essential) that the leader is paying attention to how things are progressing. They need to evaluate the individual's, or team's, performance and progress and be able to support them or correct things quickly. (The action plan, which we cover later in this chapter, will be a great help for this.)

R for REVIEWED (or REWARDED)

Many people become frustrated in their jobs because they work diligently, achieve their objectives to a greater or lesser degree, and get no feedback or response from their bosses. This step in the SMARTER model is really important for various reasons. It makes the whole thing a learning and coaching activity, it acknowledges performance and achievement, and shows the individual that the leader is paying attention and is involved. For both parties, lessons might be learned from how this objective went and these can be used for future activities and objectives.

One-minute objective setting plus

Another way of seeing objectives is the one-minute objective setting plus method. This was formulated by Blanchard and Johnson in *The One Minute Manager*. It offers a simple approach to setting objectives as a key skill for managers and leaders. The key steps are as follows:

1 Agree on your objectives. (Typically between three and seven, any more will spread attention too broadly.)

2 See what good behaviour looks like. (Define the specific behaviours relevant for the objective.)

3 Write out each of your objectives on a single sheet of paper using less than 250 words.

4   Read and re-read each objective daily, which requires only a minute or so each time you do it.

5   Take a minute at least once in a day to look at your performance

6   Check whether or not your behaviour matches your objective.

When agreeing the objectives it can be helpful to add the following structure to setting the objective:

1   What are you going to achieve? (Stated as a positive.)

2   When will you achieve it by?

3   What will you see, hear and feel when you have achieved it?

4   How will you know when you have achieved it? How will other people know?

5   What might stop or prevent you? What can you do about this?

6   What additional resources will help you to achieve your objective?

Both SMARTER objective setting and the one-minute objectives are particularly useful when setting objectives with or for individuals. They can also be used with team objectives, especially the SMARTER process. The third approach which follows can be used for either situation and is especially good when setting team objectives and involving them in the process and discussions.

Stepping up and stepping down

The third method is stepping up and stepping down. There are times when the level of the objective does not hit the spot for some individuals and will not act as a motivator. It may appear too low and simple, and does not match their drivers or values. Alternatively, it may seem to be too high and all the individual can see is something too difficult. This method of looking at objectives can address both of these potential problems and also helps to put a plan in place to work towards achieving the objective.

Stepping up

Step 1 – define the objective and outcome (make sure it is Specific).

Step 2 – work through the stepping up process, as shown in Figure 5.3, writing the responses into the boxes. Keep going with the same question as shown until you seem to reach the end of people's ideas. You are moving the objective up from the practical outcomes towards ones which are 'softer' and more aligned with people's values. For some people these will prove more motivating than the original outcome.

Step 3 – summarise what the outcome will give you, building up the emotional high of the ideas the group have contributed.

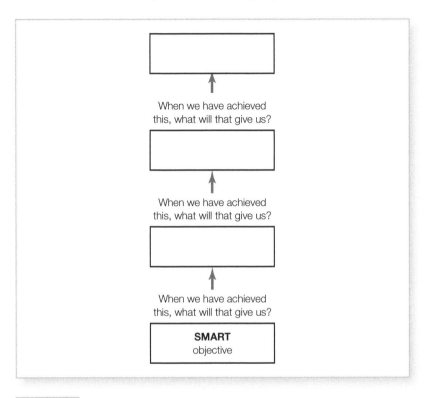

When we have achieved
this, what will that give us?

When we have achieved
this, what will that give us?

When we have achieved
this, what will that give us?

SMART
objective

figure 5.3   **Stepping up**

Stepping down

Step 1 – starting from the objective as before (see Figure 5.4), ask the first question, 'What's stopping us achieving this?' (Or 'What might stop us ?') Write the answer in the next box down.

Step 2 – move on to the question, 'What can we do about it?' Again, write the ideas into the next box.

Step 3 – repeat the questions as shown until you reach the answer 'Nothing' to what is stopping us.

Step 4 – Summarise by working back up from the bottom, emphasising each of the responses for what we can do and show how these build to the outcome, and they provide the basis for the action plan.

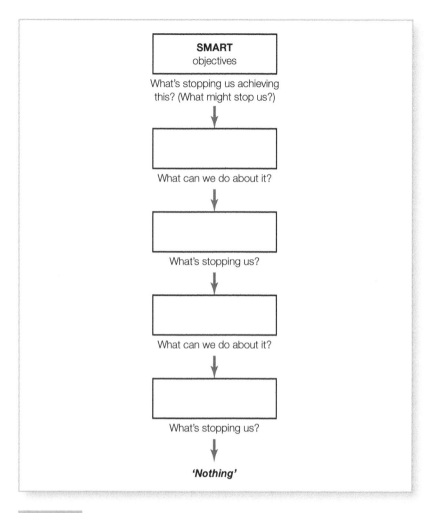

figure 5.4   Stepping down

Practice time

Reading or talking about objectives might be interesting or fun, but there is nothing like writing them down to make them more tangible.

Exercise

Think of some areas where you want to set objectives. I recommend you identify some personal ones and some for your team or business if that is relevant for you.

For the personal ones, or those for individuals in your team, use the first two options for objective setting – SMARTER and one-minute objectives.

Objective 1:

Objective 2:

Objective 3:

For any team objectives (or possibly for a personal or individual objective) work through the stepping up and down process to see how it works.

The action plan

Plans and objectives have little or no value without implementation. I am frequently surprised in organisations where I am working by how rarely managers encourage their teams or team members to have, and use, action plans for their objectives. There are many ways of doing this, and it is not important what method people use. The key is that there is an action plan for each objective. This plan is going to help the individual to achieve the objective and it will also help you to moni-tor, manage and support them in the process.

A simple way of doing this is to draw a set of steps on to a blank sheet for each objective (see Figure 5.5). Then work through identifying the steps you need to take and write them in. Put in some 'marker' dates to keep you on track and to review progress. The other two points are to note any areas of help or resources you need as well as any possible problems.

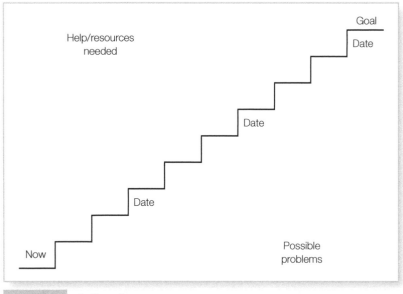

figure 5.5   Action plan

Having applied these tools to identify and set the objectives for your team, you can then use them to set the objectives for team members.

When agreeing objectives, encourage team members to write theirs using one of the methods above which will strengthen their owner-ship. It is not something that has to be added to your task list.

Make sure they write the action plan for each of their objectives and that you have a copy.

Discuss and finalise the objectives and action plans.

Put the review dates in your diary and stick to them!

Summary

- It is an essential part of the leader's role to provide the direction for their team. If you cannot give a clear direction, why will anyone follow you?
- Ideally, the direction should start with having a clear vision for your team, regardless of the type of team or level.
- Be clear about the difference between the vision and goals and objectives.
- The better you become at setting objectives the probability is you will have improved performance and productivity from your team and increased motivation from the team members.
- The principles of management by objectives are still true today and organisations which apply them are more successful.
- Correctly set objectives allow for individuals to feel a sense of achievement and also for teams to share a collective feeling of achievement when delivering on the team objectives. Many of the theories of motivation suggest this is one of the most powerful drivers for all of us.
- There is no one 'best' or 'right' way of setting objectives, although SMARTER does work.
- Practise using the different methods shown in this chapter so that you can apply them with team members for their individual objectives and with the group for the team objectives.
- Make sure there are action plans for each objective – and monitor them.

Summary – setting the direction

GOOD OBJECTIVES	INEFFECTIVE OBJECTIVES
Indicate *what* is to be achieved and *how well* it has to be done	Do not specify any standards of performance
Are *measurable* in terms of quality and quantity	Are vague and unspecific
Indicate who is primarily responsible for ensuring that it is achieved	Omit placing responsibility on anyone
Forecast an *end result or deliverable*	Describe an activity without specifying an end result
Are clear and *unambiguous*	Are open to misinterpretation
Make it clear *when* the end result is to be achieved	Are open-ended and without any time limit
Are *realistic*, i.e. *can* be achieved 100 per cent, taking all the circumstances of the situation into account, and the authority and ability of the person concerned	Are set unrealistically high, i.e. cannot be achieved in the circumstances

References

[1] Peter Drucker, *The Practice of Management*, Harper & Brothers, 1954.

[2] Robert Rodgers and John Hunter, 'Impact of Management by Objectives on Organizational Productivity', *Journal of Applied Psychology*, 1992.

[3] Robert S. Kaplan and David P. Norton, *The Strategy-Focused Organization*, Harvard Business School Press, 2001.

[4] Dr Jac Fitz-enz, *How Smart HCM Drives Financial Performance*, Workforce Intelligence Institute & Success Factors, 2006.

[5] Edwin Locke, 'Toward a Theory of Task Motivation and Incentives', *Organizational Behavior and Human Performance*, 3(3), 1968.

[6] Edwin Locke and Gary Latham, *Goal Setting: A Motivational Technique That Works*, Prentice Hall, 1984.

[7] G.T. Doran, 'S.M.A.R.T. way to write management's goals and objectives', *Management Review*, 70(11): 35–36.

6

Monitoring and controlling performance

In the previous chapter I stressed how important it is for the leader to provide the direction for the team and for individuals. This chapter looks at another activity which is equally as important and follows on from the importance of providing direction. It is one of the key functions of a leader as defined by John Adair in his book, *Action-Centred Leadership*, monitoring and controlling what is happening. Having the direction is great. It is not much use if the team is going off track, which is where so many leaders and teams slip up. For a variety of reasons they get distracted or fall behind with plans. If the leader has established the appropriate systems for monitoring and controlling performance, action can be taken quickly to correct what is happening. However, many are reluctant to act and prefer to leave things, hoping they will come right. When this happens it can be much harder to make the corrections and could even be too late.

This chapter will help you to feel more confident about introducing and using methods for monitoring and controlling what is happening – and taking action.

Monitoring performance

When introducing any system or process for monitoring performance, there are a few questions which will help you. When you visit your doctor, their question and answer approach is a good starting point to monitoring your health. They will check a number of key indicators such as height, weight, pulse and blood pressure and will then go on to more specific or detailed tests. In your role, you can apply the same principles for managing performance within your team. Questions you should ask include:

- What are the key activities I need to monitor? (The 20 per cent which drive performance rather than the 80 per cent of 'routine' tasks.)
- What are expected levels of performance for these?
- What evidence will I see, or need to see?
- How can I monitor them?
- How will the team report or communicate these activities?
- What actions will I take if we are not achieving the fundamental standards or are falling behind the plans?

In the previous chapter, 'Setting the direction for your team', the process in Figure 5.1 (reproduced here as Figure 6.1) showed how we move from establishing the vision through various stages until we have a foundation of key performance indicators (sometimes referred to as standards of performance). This is where you start to identify the activities to monitor. The other place to look is within the objectives and in the action plans. You can see that the key performance indicators are the first step. They are the foundation and underpin the behaviours and outputs for the objectives and goals.

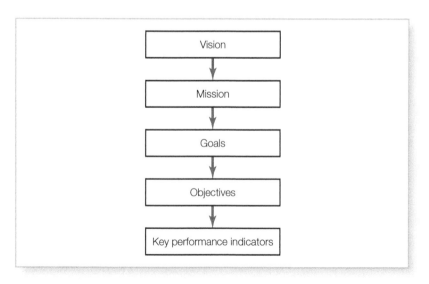

figure 6.1   Setting the direction

Setting the key performance indicators (KPIs)

There are various ways of setting these. If the team is new and the team members are inexperienced (they are probably at the 'forming' stage which was introduced in Chapter 2), it is better for you to identify and define the KPIs. When the team is further along the dynamic process ('norming' or 'performing') or the team members are reasonably experienced, it is more effective to involve them in the exercise. This helps to generate their commitment and ensures the levels suggested will be achievable.

Case study

Working with a customer and sales support team on a workshop about 'Delivering Service Excellence' we had an exercise on defining the KPIs for the function and the individuals. The syndicates presented their ideas back to the group and eventually an agreed list of activities, behaviours and measures was compiled.

Later, when we broke for lunch we were joined by the top management team. They read the list with interest and asked how the items had been decided and by whom. When told the group had done it all, the management team commented that they agreed with everything listed but said they would not have dared to suggest some of the levels identified and defined in the measures. Although impressed, they were concerned these might be too much of a stretch. We checked that the group were happy with what they had set and believed they could achieve these.

When checking three months later, these standards were being met or exceeded and customer satisfaction was improving, with complaints reduced by 30 per cent.

The areas where you set these KPIs will depend on the team you are leading and the function or department you are working in. They could cover timekeeping, absenteeism, response times, wastage, delivery schedules, customer service, costs, stock levels, standard of work and many, many more. Whatever areas you set them in, they need to be considered as a minimum acceptable level of performance. To be effective they should be:

Relevant – people need to see how these fit with their job, objectives and the team direction.

Clear – everyone can understand what is expected.

Fair – everyone knows they have to work to the same standard.

Adaptable – they can be moved up or down or reframed if people are struggling to meet them, or exceeding the original levels set.

Respected – credit is given when levels are met. They are not moved or raised without some discussion with team members.

(To be fair to you, it will take some time and experience to be able to achieve all five of these consistently.)

There are two types of KPIs or standards, quantitative and qualitative. The quantitative KPIs will have numbers or specific actions and activities connected with them. They can easily be assessed to see whether they have been achieved or not.

Examples of quantitative KPIs:

To respond to customer contact within six hours.

To produce initial reports with a maximum of three errors.

Reports to follow the agreed department template.

To make ten phone calls an hour.

The qualitative KPIs are trickier to measure or assess, because they are more subjective. However, this does not mean you avoid them. Similar to the SM of SMARTER (introduced in Chapter 5), you need to be specific with defining the KPI and this will make it easier to identify when it is being achieved.

Examples of qualitative KPIs:

To answer, and finish, phone calls with customers using the agreed style of greeting and closing.

To be prepared to contribute to meetings.

To maintain company vehicle in a clean and tidy state.

To communicate openly with fellow team members, ensuring they have all relevant information.

Arriving at the right mix and level of KPIs and standards can be challenging. A good way to start is by looking at what is expected in other departments and make yours compatible with these, while being relevant to your own team. You can also look at the following:

1   Past standards – what has been expected or established previously?

2   Estimation – calculating time required to complete tasks or of realistic workloads and deliverables.

3   Discussion with team – identifying and negotiating what is reasonable.

4   Best practice – checking what is considered best practice, using other organisations or teams to benchmark against.

5 Instinct – hunches or guesswork about what could or should be achieved.

Taking time to identify the range of appropriate KPIs for your team will be time well spent. When the team know what is expected, and this is made clear, it becomes easier to get them to move on to setting objectives. Having clear standards is something many people like. Being clear about expectations can prevent future problems and also can contribute to a sense of pride from belonging to a team with high standards. Rather than approaching this in a random manner, although that is an option, especially if doing this with the team, it can help your thinking to group the KPIs into different areas.

Exercise

Think of your team and identify the areas where you can set KPIs using the headings shown. Start with identifying the areas to set them and when completed go back and think about what level you want to pitch them at and define those.

Quantitative

Operational – job outputs:

For example: To make 20 outbound calls per shift.

Administration elements:

For example: To submit weekly reports accurately and with fewer than two errors.

Personal and interpersonal (individual actions, behaviour, etc. and interactions with others):

For example: To respond to, or acknowledge, colleagues' e-mails or requests within two hours.

Qualitative

Operational – job outputs:

For example: To respond to customers' queries using one of the established departmental templates.

Administration elements:

For example: To ensure documentation is filed appropriately using the agreed system and on the day it is produced.

Personal and interpersonal (individual actions, behaviour, etc. and interactions with others):

For example: To listen to colleagues and customers without interruption.

As mentioned, these KPIs can become the baseline from which the team, and team members, work towards achieving their objectives. They are not set in stone. There is room for some flexibility in how you use them. You can reduce or lower the level for newcomers who need to develop their skills in their role and use the baseline as an objective for the individuals to achieve. If the team are performing well, you might want to raise the bar and increase the target level for the KPIs, which lifts the overall expectation of what the team can deliver. What they do provide is the foundation for your monitoring.

The three steps for monitoring and controlling performance

The steps in the 'PEA' process, shown below, can help to clarify the purpose of monitoring and controlling performance and why it should not happen in isolation. As it shows, the three phases are used in sequence – there is a before, during and after. However, as the leader you may have to use all of them simultaneously because not all of your team members will be in the same phase at the same time. You need to stay aware of this so that you are on top of things; overlooking any one of them can cause problems for the individual and overall performance.

As I have emphasised in this chapter and the previous one, it is your responsibility as the leader to make sure the 'plan' elements are put in place before the team can get on with whatever they are expected to do. Without them you cannot monitor performance with any consistency or objectivity. The elements within each step are not in any particular sequence or order of importance. They do all need to be considered and established. After the plan elements are in place, 'execution' is the next stage. Some of your team will do a good job, some only an average one and possibly some will make mistakes or underperform. The final column, 'after', is really important. Unfortunately, it is one which many managers and leaders overlook or only use bits of. Too often the most frequent reaction after the execution stage is the first one, ignoring what people have done whether it is successful or slightly off the mark. This 'no response' consequence is counter-productive because it leaves people in the dark about their performance. Should they keep going at their current level or improve? In behavioural terms, one of the worst things you can do is to ignore people and not tell them how they are doing.

Plan	*Execution*	*After*
What you do before performance	What team and individuals actually do and deliver	What happens after performance
Clarity of roles and responsibilities	*Achieve the baseline levels of KPIs*	*Stay quiet – they are expected to achieve*
Establishing KPIs	*Work through action plans of objectives*	*Criticise performance*
Setting clear objectives		*Give praise*
Defining monitoring and control processes	*Miss targets*	*Provide constructive feedback*
	Slip behind KPI levels	

A major benefit of having clearly stated KPIs and action plans which include review dates is that there are a number of points where you, the leader, can check how someone is doing, and whether they are on course or slipping. This means that you cannot use the 'ignore' or 'no response' option.

If the individual is not meeting the KPI or is falling behind on their action plan you need to make an assessment before jumping in. What is the reason for this? Is it because they can't do it or is it that they won't do it? If it is 'can't do' please do not criticise or reprimand: far too often this is the reaction of many managers. Give support, coach or organise training to help the individual develop the necessary skills. If that will not work, maybe they need to be given another task or role. If the reason for underachievement is 'won't do', i.e. an attitude issue, then it is time to reprimand.

The key for the 'after' column is to make sure you are looking for opportunities to give feedback on behaviour and performance. Rather than focusing on areas of underperformance or underachievement, spend more time catching people 'doing something right' (attributed to Bill Marriott Snr, who built the hotel group). After all, the majority of people you are leading will be doing 98 per cent of their job right, which is what you want to encourage and keep them doing. Most people approach their work with a simple set of requirements:

Tell me what I am expected to do.

Give me the right tools and support to do the job.

Tell me how I am doing.

Reward me appropriately.

It is not that difficult to do as a manager or leader when you look at it this way.

The planning–control cycle

Although this is shown as a cycle (see Figure 6.2) it is most effective when used both ways.

Backwards: Compare actual events with the planned – then review and revise the targets where necessary. Learn from successes as well as from any underachievements.

Forwards: To establish any extra activities or resources required to attain the existing targets.

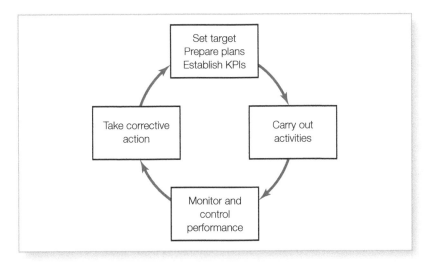

figure 6.2 The planning-control cycle

Effective controls

When you have established the KPIs or standards for your team and have the basis to monitor against, you need to consider how you can control the performance of the team. Many leaders are uncomfortable with the concept of controlling people and their work. This is frequently an underlying cause of project deadlines being missed, team targets not being achieved or individuals not delivering on their objectives. Yet, as a leader your role is to see that objectives are met and control is an essential part of this. Effective controls are used to assess whether the agreed direction is being maintained and, if not, the extent of the variance from the plan. There should be nothing to fear from identifying and implementing controls because they can be good for all concerned.

Effective controls combined with directing your resources into the right activities can be a major factor in the success of any leader or manager. Controls are not intended to be used for policing purposes and this must be understood by your team. The only individuals who need to worry about controls as a policing tool are those who are not doing their job properly or honestly. If you are facing this situation, controls and using them effectively will be your friends and will help you to tackle the individual.

Good controls should allow the following:

1   Comparisons of achievement versus plan.
2   A factual basis for assessing key performance indicators.
3   An indication of development needs, both individual and team.
4   A basis for fair comparison of individuals and teams.
5   Early warning of variances which require corrective action.

A good control system offers even more benefits for you and the team. Without control a lot of planning might be wasted as you would not know if you were on course to achieve objectives.

- You can get the best return from your resources.
- Control makes sure you are consistently working towards the team's objectives.
- KPIs and standards reduce reasons for arguments. Monitoring enables you to be organised and systematic in correcting performance.
- Effective controls can help the team feel more confident and together.
- You can stay on top of forecasting and planning with the right controls.
- Effective controls enable team members to assess their own performance and adapt if needed. This can create more commitment and greater job satisfaction.

The more complex the team's task, or the longer the term, the more necessary the controls and their application. Imagine you are the pilot of a plane setting off on a long-haul flight from London to Kuala Lumpur. After all of the pre-flight checks you hand over to your co-pilot to take charge. Unfortunately, they set the course 1° out. By the time you should be reaching Kuala Lumpur how many hundreds of miles are you away from your destination? (See Figure 6.3.)

If you let this go without any controls in place, when will you realise you are off course? More worrying is the question, 'Where are we?' You would not know which direction to head in, whether you have sufficient fuel or what alternative airports you could aim for.

However, supposing you had implemented controls from just after take-off, checking that you are on course over various European cities, then others *en route*. If you discovered any slippage, how difficult is it to make the necessary change? It will take a lot less fuel, effort and worry!

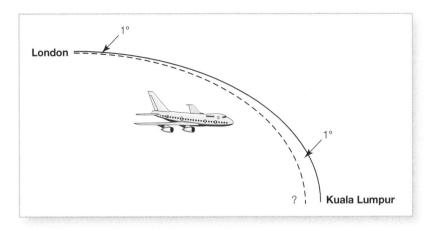

figure 6.3   **Keeping on course**

When thinking about your team you need to ask yourself, 'What can I use to control my team and their performance or activities?', 'What specific actions, behaviours or outcomes will help me?', 'Which of these can be in my "early warning" list?'

Typically, your controls will fall into several distinct areas, which can be thought of as the 'whats' and the 'wheres' of measurement. They will tell you exactly how people are performing against plans and provide you with information to take corrective action. These are the main areas: fundamental performance against the KPIs; observed behaviours and actions; discussion with team members; feedback from other functions or sources; figures and statistics; progress against project or personal action plans.

Having worked out the 'what' areas to control, and 'where' they will occur, the challenge is to find the best 'how' to do it. Effective control systems need to be easy to understand for the leader and the team members. The system should allow the leader and the individuals to easily see how things are progressing and identify any shortfalls or potential issues. Any sort of written (or IT) reporting needs to be easy to complete and to read.

Using the control options

Written controls will usually be reports. These might be reporting progress against agreed plans and they will outline successes or any shortfalls. Ideally they should have space to give reasons for any issues and to list the next actions to remedy these. The frequency will vary depending on the scope of the activities and dates for completion of the objective. My suggestion is that the shorter the reporting time-scales the better. (Think back to the plane example.) The quicker you can take corrective action the fewer problems in adjusting the behaviour and performance. The table below gives a suggestion for a simple report format. If you have an experienced team to lead, it is a good idea to involve them in developing a system which will work for all of you.

Sample of simple report (add as many rows as you need)

Date	Activity, outcome or KPI	Result	Reason	Implications or actions

Describe the activity or task that had to be accomplished. Then state the result – missed, achieved, by how much? Give a brief description of the reason, whether a success or a miss. The final column is to encourage some thoughts about what can be learned from this and what needs to be done.

An even better control mechanism is to have a plan, combined with the report shown above. The forward plan, below, provides a basis against which you can control performance. Define the main actions or activities to be done. How will you measure success or achievement? 'Dependencies' is asking the person to think who or what else needs to happen in order to achieve the task. Finally, identify whether help or support is needed and where to get it.

Date	Actions for next week/ month	Measure	Dependencies	Help or support needed

Within project teams the control process is essential and should cover all milestones. Many projects miss their end deadlines. The reasons for this are usually not about poor management or performance in the latter stages of the project. Problems start earlier and slippage happens because of poor control and a reluctance to take corrective action. Good project plans and systems will have elements built in to them which can be helpful for controlling performance.

When individuals and the team have clear objectives, one of your principal means of control is using the action plans. If done properly, as covered in Chapter 5, the action plan would cover the tasks and show key dates along the way, which provide interim deadlines for both you and the individual to review progress. These dates must go into your diary and meetings should be arranged to review progress. Once the team realise these are going to happen (and be constructive) they will work towards them more consistently. These reviews become part of your control system and you can monitor progress and performance at them. They provide you with the opportunity to correct any underperformance where appropriate or to encourage more of the same when things are going well.

Many leaders find it difficult to use observed behaviours as a control process. When they see someone not behaving in the right way or not meeting some KPIs or standards, many leaders do not feel confident or comfortable in addressing it. There are a number of reasons for this. Starting with the most basic, they do not know how to approach the situation in a constructive way. They may be concerned that their message will be taken wrongly or lead to some level of conflict. Another reason can be that the leader is feeling annoyed or irritated by what they are seeing and realise that this is not a good state in which to handle things, because they may not handle the situation constructively.

When seeing some behaviour that is not appropriate or within the agreed standards, the key is to address it in a timely manner. This might not be immediately, because the circumstances may not be appropriate. As soon as you can, see the individual where you can talk quietly and privately. Be clear about what you observed and describe it specifically. Staying calm, describe what you want the person to start doing differently and explain why. Check that they understand and that they will do it. If there is any problem, establish the reason and deal with it by offering more support or development.

You can use discussion with individuals or the whole team as a control mechanism too. An interactive session with the right questions can help people to see things they may be overlooking, such as patterns or trends. Another option is to use data or figures, either ones produced in the organisation or those you collect as the leader. The concept of an effective control system is to find the most useful and applicable mix of methods for your team and particular situation. It will be even more useful if it is transparent and clearly understood by all.

❝ Controls are purely a means to an end. The end is control.

Peter Drucker[1]

Summary

- Learn to feel comfortable with the whole area of monitoring and controlling performance. A key part of your role as a leader is to be able to let the team and the individuals know how they are doing against objectives and the direction you set.

- Take time to identify the areas which make a difference to performance. (Consider Pareto's 80–20 principle – in which 20 per cent contribute 80 per cent of the output or deliverables.) The objectives and KPIs within these areas should be the first ones you look to monitor and control.

- Define the KPIs or standards of performance clearly. The quantitative ones are fairly easy; the qualitative ones need to be explicit to avoid misunderstandings and misinterpretation.

- Consider involving the team in defining the KPIs and the control processes if they are experienced. You are more likely to get their commitment if you can do this.

- When you are clear about the objectives for the team and individuals plus the KPIs, you can identify what are the elements of these which you can use for your control process. When these are clear, work out how you can control performance most effectively.

- Remember, effective control systems need to be clear, simple and transparent. They should be beneficial for all concerned so that everyone knows how their performance is against plans and expectations.

- Act quickly to correct performance – remember the risk with the flight plan even if it is only 1° off course.

- Setting the direction for the team is of limited value if you do not act to keep the team and individuals on track to achieve the objectives.

Reference

[1] Peter Drucker, *Management: tasks, responsibilities, practices*, HarperBusiness, 1993.

7

Communicating with your team

Getting your communication right can be the greatest challenge for many leaders. Whenever I ask groups for examples of good behaviour from good leaders, invariably it is communication that features high on the list. The issue with communicating with your team is that you need to be able to adapt your communication style to suit the needs of the individuals, the group and the situation. When we were looking at Action Centred Leadership in Chapter 4, we saw that you have to consider the team and the individual. In this chapter we will consider a number of aspects of communication, including the processes involved, reducing barriers and how to improve your listening. This latter point is as vital as your ability to express yourself clearly.

Effective communication is essential for the team to succeed and for organisational success. As a leader, your role is fundamentally all about communicating – with your team, colleagues and peer group, senior managers and externally.

What is communication?

Most of us take communication for granted. After all, it is just something we do and most of the time we do it without thinking. In reality, how many people do you know who you would consider a good communicator? If we were all so good, why do so many errors occur and misunderstandings happen in all areas of life? Arguably, the majority of problems can be linked back to poor communication.

Communication can be defined as the sharing of information between two or more individuals or groups to reach a common understanding (it is not necessary to agree with each other to achieve this). When giving or receiving incomplete information, what is the result? With only a partial understanding, problems will occur.

Let us look at what happens when we are communicating (see Figure 7.1).

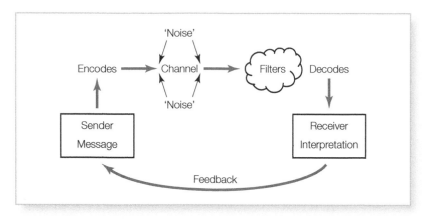

figure 7.1   **The communication process**

Working through this process:

1 The sender decides they have a message to send.

2 The sender 'encodes' their message, i.e. puts it into words, pictures, etc.

3 They transmit through the 'channel' they have chosen. Face to face, telephone, e-mail, notice board or any other medium.

4 The channel has to handle 'noise'. This is a bit of jargon and means anything that interferes with the channel and message or distracts from it.

5 The message reaches the 'filters' of the receiver(s), which will influence their perception and, therefore, affect their decoding.

6 The receiver interprets the message they have decoded.

7 The receiver provides feedback. They may do this verbally, through questions or acknowledgement and statements. Alternatively, it could be non-verbal with gestures, expressions or changes in posture. (If using e-mail or other written media the feedback can also be in writing.)

Stages 1 to 6 combine to make up one-way communication. That is, the sender transmits, the receiver gets the message and there is no feedback response to the sender. This presents a challenge for the sender. As Figure 7.2 shows, the sender sends an intended message (I), but it is received differently (R). It is subjected to the 'Arc of Distortion'. The art of the good communicator is to make this arc as small an angle as possible – and not so bad that the received message is obtuse, when the arc goes over 90°.

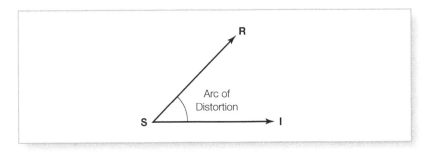

figure 7.2   **The arc of distortion**

Communication will usually be improved when it is two-way.

Looking at the process we can start to identify where communication can go wrong:

1   The sender might fail to think about the objectives of their message or not consider the receiver and their possible reaction to the message or their ability to understand it.

2   The encoding could be a significant contributor to communication problems. Pitching the message at the wrong level, making it too complicated or even too simple are just some of the possible errors that can occur at this stage. This usually happens because the sender puts their focus on their message rather than on the receiver.

3   The next possible barrier or problem area is with the channel. Is it the most effective for the message? How many times do we hear about people using e-mail rather than going to talk to a colleague, or picking up the phone?

4   Although a lot of factors which contribute to 'noise' and interfere with the channel might be outside the sender's control, having an awareness of them and taking action to minimise those which you can control or influence will help.

5   The 'filters' can certainly be a barrier in the process. These are unique to each individual and, to make things worse, can keep changing according to the person's mood of the moment! The 'filters' influence the receiver's view or opinion of the sender and the message. A thought to remember for this barrier is 'perception is reality'. The individual receiver is not wrong if their perception does not match your message.

6   The decoding can also be a barrier depending on what has come through the 'filters' and the receiver's perception combined with their understanding of the message. The other factor influencing decoding is the receiver's comprehension of the actual words used and whether they have the right vocabulary.

7   The feedback loop should help to improve the process, but it does not always work. Receivers do not always tell the sender that they have not understood the message and, to make it worse, will often say they do even when they do not. (There are a variety of reasons why many of us are reluctant to admit our lack of understanding.) The sender is not always attentive enough to pick up signals from the receiver, so they overlook the feedback or only choose to see or hear what they want to.

When you think about each of the potential barriers and problem areas it is no surprise that communication goes wrong as often as it does. However, with some thought and application you can make sure that this happens less frequently within your own situation and with your team.

Another definition for communication

Many years ago some delegates on a workshop I was running provided a definition for communication I have used ever since. 'To understand and to be understood.' The simplicity of this, coupled with its accuracy, is what appeals to me. Think about it in the context of your own communication and work through each part.

'To understand' – what are the elements you need to understand? The objective or purpose of your message is part of it. The other, which is equally, or possibly more, important is to think about the receiver and their level of understanding and likely attitude towards you and the message. These two need to happen almost simultaneously.

'To be understood' – using the information from the first stage you can plan and structure your message, using the most effective delivery channel to maximise the chance of it being understood.

Alongside this definition, another really useful thought to carry with you is: *The meaning of my communication is the response I get.* (This is what is called a presupposition from NLP, or Neuro Linguistic Programming.) Taking responsibility for how your communication is received and the response you get is both empowering and challenging. By doing this you avoid blaming others for not reacting or behaving in the way you expect or hope. It can reduce your frustration, whilst making you take ownership for the outcome, which means you need to think about what you want to transmit as a message and how you will do it (especially in non-verbal terms).

Planning communication

You can help your communication by planning carefully. Ask the following questions:

WHY am I communicating?

- What do I want someone else to do as a result of my communication?
- If I am just passing information, rather than stimulating someone to do something, why do they need this information?

WHO is the receiver?

- What is their background?
- What is their attitude?
- What do they already know about the subject?
- What language will they understand (think of jargon as a language too)?
- What do they expect me to communicate?

WHAT is the message?

- Should I start with an 'overview' to put the message into context, to give a good reason for making the communication?
- What are the main points?
- What is the logical sequence, building on the receiver's existing knowledge?
- How can I end so as to indicate the action I want to see as a result?

HOW should I communicate?

- Is the situation formal or informal?
- Is speed important?
- Is there a lot of detail to be transmitted accurately?

- Is persuasion involved?
- Which channel or medium will work best?

HOW can I get feedback?

- What response do I need to get?
- How can I check understanding?
- What can I do to make it easier for the receiver to give me feedback?

The final question can be the toughest to achieve. If you are not getting any feedback or obvious response think back to 'the meaning of my communication is the response I get'. You may think you are open and approachable, but that might not be how others perceive you based on your behaviour. It could also be that you have not picked up some signals or other response. Good communicators will pay attention to their receivers. Not only listening to what they say, both words and tone, but also looking at how they are behaving and reacting.

How to make communication two-way

- Think about your receiver(s) and their likely attitudes to the message and probable response.
- Put yourself in their shoes, show you empathise with them.
- Build rapport.
- Observe, and listen to, the response.
- Be flexible and willing to change the way you communicate.
- Encourage feedback and response – with the right behaviour and questions. Avoid criticising any response, curb any impatience, reassure and answer as honestly as you can.

" Nothing beats personal, two-way communication for fostering cooperation and teamwork and for building an attitude of trust and understanding among employees.

Bill Packard, Co-Founder, Hewlett Packard

Being a good role model

The way you communicate with your team can have a significant impact on their performance, morale and personal interactions. You should not underestimate your power as a role model and the example you will set for your team (and others in the organisation). Some ways you can achieve this are shown below.

Openness in attitude and behaviour

Openness is the key for effective communication in the workplace. Encouraging open channels of communication and sharing generates active participation and collaboration as well as creating an environment for resolving conflicts.

Communicate expectations

Clearly state your expectations with your team. This way minimises misunderstandings. Team members do not have to guess whether they are doing the right thing. Communicate your expectations visually and orally where possible.

Act proactively

Be visible to your team, do not stay behind your desk. Go to them, listen to them. MBWA (management by wandering about) improves communication and morale, encourages an open culture and makes you appear more approachable. It also enables you to spot any problems early.

Communicate positively

Look for opportunities to emphasise the good news, the successes and acknowledge achievements through regular one-to-one feedback and team meetings.

Be a good, or great, listener

Perhaps the most difficult part of communication is effective listening. As Dale Carnegie said many years ago in *How to Win Friends and Influence People,* 'You will make twice as many friends in a day by listening as you will by speaking.'[1] More on this later!

Communication networks in organisations

The pathways along which information flows throughout an organisation are called communication networks. As a leader you will be operating within a range of different communication networks. Some of these networks will be within your team, others will have an impact on your team or your team may affect the network. One of the challenges for you as a leader is to recognise the different communication networks you are involved with and understand how you need to act within each.

Although the core skills will be common within each network, there can be subtle variations that you, or your team members, need to be aware of. Typical communication networks are shown in Figure 7.3, with you, the leader, being A. The arrows show the lines of communication and indicate that it can, or should, be two-way.

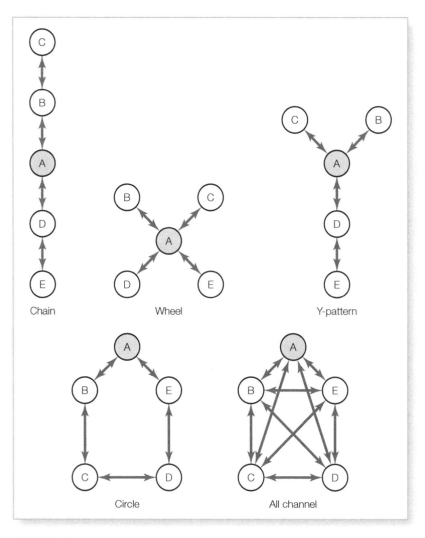

figure 7.3   Communication networks

There is not necessarily a best option amongst these. The type of communication network that works for your team will depend on the nature of the tasks and the extent to which members need to communicate with each other to achieve group goals. Circumstances will influence which is going to be the most effective. However, it is going to be more helpful if you can get the team to use the 'all channel' network. This shows that there is more direct communication between the team members without always going via you, which will allow for more sharing of ideas and information and can reduce conflict and personality clashes.

How to communicate as the sender

Within each network, your role in the communication process is vital. Your power as a role model of good communication is key. You need to transmit clear, understandable messages. Being able to express yourself appropriately for your team members and for all those you communicate with outside your team is important. When sending your messages, remember the KISS principle: Keep It Short and Simple, irrespective of the channel you are using. Over-elaboration, too much explanation or using vocabulary beyond your receiver are just some of the things that can lead to misunderstanding and poor communication.

On pages 93–4 I listed some questions to ask when planning communication. By asking yourself these questions you will find they help you focus on planning and structuring your message. This will help improve the quality and effectiveness of what you transmit. However, the words you use will only contribute a small percentage of the impact of your message. In a face-to-face situation non-verbal elements are the large majority. These include voice tone, pitch, tempo and volume. The other significant part is your body language. Between them, these send out many messages within your message. Receivers will pay attention to the various signals and make judgements about your confidence, integrity and truthfulness, belief in your message, attitude towards them and many other aspects.

Using body language

Many of the elements of our body language are used unconsciously and can be hard to alter or control. A number are genetic, many are cultural and others we develop as we grow up. It can be useful to have an awareness of your own body language traits so that you can identify elements you might want to change or refine.

You can help yourself by raising your awareness of some key aspects of body language and how you can utilise them to help to improve your effectiveness as a leader and communicator. We often forget that our appearance is a part of the message we send and influences people's perception of us. Make sure yours is appropriate for the environment and situation you are in. Many workplaces have relaxed dress codes to smart or business casual, so avoid wearing a suit and tie unless you need to do so because of a client meeting or something similar. Whether we like it or not, we are all inclined to make snap judgements based on subjective first impressions. Our appearance plays a large part in this. Do not stand out for the wrong reasons.

Within body language there is a subset called 'proxemics'. This is about the space zones or personal reaction bubbles we have around us (see Figure 7.4). There are four of these zones and we unconsciously accept people into the appropriate one depending on our relationship with the person. If someone does move in too close we feel as though they are 'invading our space'. When this happens we feel uncomfortable, possibly crowded and even intimidated. Where possible we will look to move to increase the distance until it feels right.

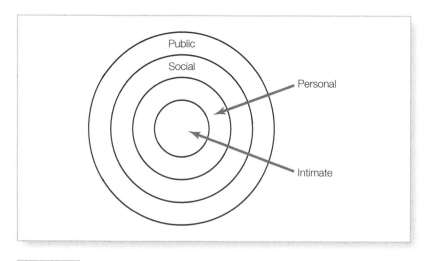

figure 7.4   'Proxemic' zones

The 'typical' distances for each zone are as follows:

> Intimate zone – from immediately next to us out to about 18 inches or 45cm. The only people we are happy to let into this space will be those who are close to us and where we do not mind accidental physical contact.

Personal zone – from 18 inches or 50cm out to 4 ft or 120cm. This is for close friends, family members or those with whom we feel more trust exists or is developing.

Social zone – from 4ft or 120cm to 12 ft or 3.5m. This covers most of our interactions, with acquaintances and colleagues, suppliers and customers. Positioning within this zone is an indication of the closeness of the relationship.

Public zone – beyond 12ft or 3.5m. Where speaking to groups or dealing with those where there is little or no relationship, nor any need for one.

These distances are generalities and do change according to cultures and even individuals' upbringing. Those brought up in urban environments might shrink these dimensions by 50 per cent, and this could apply to a number of cultures around the world.

Why does this matter to your leadership? Be aware of your team members' needs for space and how it might vary. Be careful not to get too close and crowd them. Also, do not be too distant. Literally, 'keeping your distance' might make the other people feel you are too remote and treating them from the public zone or beyond. Think about this when team members come to your desk and where you position chairs and the distance this creates. What happens if you are going to them? Position yourself in the right zone for the team member, not your comfort zone.

The third major aspect to consider is your overall posture and the messages you send through this. Standing tall will influence your mood and your voice projection. It helps if you breathe properly and deeply too. All of these combine to make you appear more confident. When with your team, look them in the eye, keep your gaze level and be aware of your gestures. These should be natural, but do make sure you are not sending conflicting messages – for example, if your hands are making chopping or pointing movements when trying to talk in a measured tone! Be careful if you like to have a pen or another object in your hand. Movements will appear exaggerated and will attract unconscious attention from others, and make any 'leakage' more obvious. (This term refers to the way our extremities can betray our real feelings.)

The combination of words, tone and body language make up your message. You may hope that receivers will be consciously attending to what you are saying but unconsciously they are receiving many of the other signals and calibrating these against the words. If they all appear to be fitting together, then the message is consistent and has power and impact. Should any of the non-verbal or body language signals appear to be out of sync with the words, the message starts being diluted and the receiver will look for more mismatches. People prioritise these signals over the words you are using. Basically, the HOW of your delivery is as important (or arguably, more important) than WHAT you are delivering.

You as the receiver

> ❝ We've all heard the criticism, 'He talks too much.' When was the last time you heard someone criticized for listening too much?'
>
> *Norm Augustine, Former CEO, Lockheed Martin*

The flip side of your communication with your team is your role as a receiver. If you are going to create a climate for open communication you also need to be a great role model as a receiver. A large part of this will come from how your team feel they can approach you, how receptive and responsive you are, and how you behave towards them.

Exercise: How good a listener are you?

1 When a problem arises at work, do you often react before gathering all the facts?

2 At meetings, once you have made your presentation or statement do you have a tendency to switch off?

3 Do you often finish statements for the slow deliberate talker in the interest of saving time?

4 Do you often reword sentences or find yourself correcting words people use while they are in conversation with you?

5 Do you find yourself concentrating more on the *way* people say things (grammatically, or the words they use) than on the content or message they are trying to put across?

6 Do you find yourself interrupting others?

7 Are you often so busy thinking of what you are going to say next that you stop listening to the other person in the meantime?

8 Are you talking more than listening?

9 Do you always feel the need to fill a pause in conversation?

10 Do you often fake listening and daydream instead?

11 Are you hesitant in asking questions to clarify your understanding of something being said?

12 Do you find yourself looking everywhere but at the person talking to you?

If your answer is yes to any of these questions, you have room for improvement in your listening.

There are some techniques or skills you can use to help others to feel you are listening to them. However, I believe that listening is fundamentally an attitude. Without this, the techniques have little or no value. If you look at the questions above, the responses are based on your attitudes rather than any skills deficiency.

Barriers to listening

Concentration wanders

We listen several times faster than most people speak. So we sometimes become bored, and our mind wanders and looks for ideas to fill in the time.

Closed mind

When we disagree with ideas or the people expressing them our minds can become closed to most of what they are saying. We then stop listening.

Failing to understand

When a speaker conveys information which we do not understand our minds tune out and we do not ask, so we stay with the information that we can assimilate easily.

We know where this is going

If something we hear triggers off an idea which we want to express we are so anxious to do so that we stop listening to what is being said.

Waiting for our turn to speak

Either we think we know where this is going, or something is said we want to build on, so we stop paying attention and miss the latter part of what is said.

Remaining silent

Because our early training taught us to remain silent while others were speaking, we forget that listening is an active process which often calls for questioning the speaker to seek clarification.

Missing key phrases

Often we listen to the general sense of what is being said but overlook the significance of key words and phrases.

Side tracked by the speaker or events

This can happen because of the speaker's non-verbal signals, their voice or any other habit that distracts us. Other external factors can also lead to this barrier.

The four stages of effective listening

1 **Hearing** The ears sense sound waves.

2 **Interpretation** This leads to understanding or misunderstanding.

3 **Evaluation** Weighing the information and deciding how to use it.

4 **Reaction** Adopting whatever action (or inaction) we have decided on.

To be a good, or great, listener you need to make the other person feel that you are focusing on them and that they are the centre of your attention. Bearing in mind what we mentioned earlier about body language and its impact on our messages, this is equally true as a receiver. Your posture, amount of eye contact and other non-verbal signals will go a long way to letting someone know you are listening. Stop whatever else you are doing and direct your attention to the speaker, e.g. look away from your computer screen, do not read that text message. Allow them to finish before commenting or responding.

Listening requires discipline, concentration and intensive practice. Listening means understanding what others are saying. It is an active, not a passive, process and to become good listeners we must control our intellect, our emotions and our behaviour.

Developing your active listening

Although your attitude is the fundamental requirement, it can by reinforced by using some of the following techniques when listening. They contribute to what is referred to as 'active' listening, which lets the speaker know and realise you are engaged in what they are saying.

GIVING ATTENTION	*Make time to listen. Give attention and show it (by nodding, maintaining eye contact, etc.).*
WITHHOLDING COMMENT	*Let the other person finish – often the key thing is said in the last few words.*
CHECKING BACK	*Try to re-state what the other person just said. Use their words as far as possible; they can check that what you heard is what they meant.*

CLARIFYING	*Summarise what you understood to be the main points, to check understanding.*
BUILDING ON	*Develop the other person's argument or position. This is not a technique for knocking down their ideas and substituting yours!*
SHOWING SUPPORT	*Express your interest and encourage the speaker to continue.*
STRUCTURING	*Help the speaker to develop their ideas. Summarising and agreeing the main points before moving on can be a very useful idea.*

When to use different types of communication

Face to face

As an effective leader you will almost certainly find that this is how you spend most of your time and also how you get your messages across most clearly. Whether you are with the team as a whole or meeting on a one-to-one basis you are still in the best environment for two-way communication. Face-to-face communication provides immediate feedback and is potentially the best information medium because of the many channels available through voice, eye contact, posture, facial expression and other body language. It is the medium for delegation, coaching, disciplining, instructing, sharing information, answering questions, checking progress towards objectives and developing and maintaining interpersonal relations. Leaders also spend face-to-face time communicating with their managers and colleagues.

Your face-to-face time can be informal or formal. Most of it should be at the informal end of the scale, when you are wandering around and talking with team members or when they come to you with ideas, suggestions, questions or problems. The formal time will generally be when you have team meetings. Occasionally, you may be having a formal one-to-one with a team member, although this might have some slightly more serious objectives. The team meetings can be a good place to demonstrate your communication effectiveness and expertise. You can also use team meetings to develop the communication skills across your team by being adaptable in the structure of the meeting and your own approach.

Team meetings

To make team meetings more effective consider using some, or all, of these:

- Vary their frequency – the 'regular' Monday meeting or similar can become too routine and mundane.
- Have some with agendas, and some with a free structure to encourage discussion.
- Let others take the chair some of the time and you act as part of the team.
- Set some basic rules to encourage contributions: everyone has to let colleagues finish speaking – no interruptions or speaking over; no criticism of individuals only of ideas; if criticising an idea the person has to suggest an alternative.
- If you have a virtual team, or some remote team members, there are fewer opportunities for face-to-face communication. However, technology can assist with the increase of webcams and various sites and programs which can be used to communicate while seeing each other. Although not as effective as meeting in person, it is usually more effective than just using the telephone or e-mail.

Communicating via the telephone

The telephone still has a part to play in communicating with your team and other people. If you have team members who are remote from you or their colleagues, the telephone has plenty of good applications. It can be used in a timely way, with a degree of immediacy if required. It is possible to be succinct or have a lengthy conversation. The downside of not having the visual clues and cues is that this can cause misunderstandings. However, with careful planning of your message and attentive listening these can be reduced. If you have created the right environment within your team the individuals can feel comfortable telephoning you or each other. If using the telephone to pass on information keep it short and to the point. It is also good for checking progress on activities and for making people feel involved.

Written communication

This channel should be the least used within your team. It is most likely to be in the form of e-mail, although many of the same advantages and disadvantages apply for hard copy letters or other documents. Written communication can be personalised to individuals or provide the same message to the whole team simultaneously. It does have the benefit of providing a record that a message was sent. However, there are some limitations. It is difficult to convey the right degree of emotion in the message, and because you cannot influence or control what is happening for the receiver when they read it, you do not know what their reaction might be. Getting feedback is not always easy or even possible.

If you are going to use this channel, take time to think through and plan your message and the specific wording you want to use. Write it out in draft and, if time permits, leave it for a while and then reread it to check it is saying what you want in the way you want.

Use of technology in communication

We are in a radical age as far as technology and its impact on communication is concerned. The rapid spread of computer technology through laptops, tablets and smartphones has had a significant effect on most organisations and individuals. We find it almost impossible to be out of reach of these devices. On the one hand, they mean you can keep in contact with your team quickly and easily, and them with you. On the other hand, the technology can lead to unrealistic expectations of each other because we look for messages to be acknowledged or dealt with at once. Priorities are skewed in favour of urgency.

However, used properly, technology can be an asset to your communication with your team. As mentioned earlier, e-mail can be a great help although it does work better if you have some guidelines about e-mail etiquette. The options for using forms of video conferencing or web meetings can be a time and cost saver if they reduce travel and help to keep some form of face-to-face communication.

Depending on the structure and role of your team, social media can be useful. Setting up your own group within Facebook or LinkedIn can be a good way to share information or messages within your team. It is also possible to do a similar thing with Twitter, although the 140 character limit may restrict what it is used for. Another option is to set up a team 'group' for sending SMS messages to everyone at once.

Summary

- Effective communication does not just happen!
- Use the simple definition – 'To understand and to be understood' – as your approach to communicating. Think about your receivers at the same time as you are deciding on the outcome or purpose of your message. This improves the probability of you encoding it well and getting your message across clearly.

- Be a great role-model communicator for your team. Your behaviour will influence theirs. They can follow your example and improve their communication and this will lead to even better performance from the team.

- Be proactive in your communication. Keep the team informed about things as soon as you can, give them feedback on performance and share progress or setbacks promptly.

- Engage the team by asking for ideas and input. Use questions rather than statements.

- Remember, listening is an attitude first, reinforced by some skills. Work on developing your listening capability. The better you become, the more your team are likely to come to you of their own accord. This is good feedback to let you know that your communication is working well.

Reference

[1] Dale Carnegie, *How to Win Friends and Influence People*, Simon and Schuster, 1936.

8

Getting the most from your team

A significant part of your role as a leader is to get the most from the people in your team. This is often seen as a daunting challenge by many inexperienced leaders. They hope that the individuals in their team will get on and do their jobs well if left to do so. Even if they are doing so, you should be thinking about how you can get even more from them in terms of their performance and contribution. This chapter will give you some understanding and ideas for how you can achieve this and reduce any concerns you may have about doing so. You will have a better awareness of how to create the right conditions for your team to be motivated to achieve. You will recognise the importance of developing individuals and identify the different options which can be used, especially what you can provide through effective coaching and making it part of your day-to-day work with your team. To support, or reinforce, the improvements you need to think about how you can reward the individual in the most appropriate way.

Motivation

Over the years a great deal has been written about the whole area of motivation with many different theories emerging. These have tended to evolve as our understanding of people and psychology has increased. Another factor influencing motivation is the changing nature of organisations and also society, with Generation Y or the Millennial Generation group forming more of the workforce and bringing their expectations. They are perceived as wanting things to happen more quickly, expecting to be given more opportunities for growth or promotion in shorter timescales, and having less perseverance with tasks. These views may be true for some younger people, but they are unfair generalisations for many.

What is motivation? The root of the word is medieval Latin, 'Motivus' – 'serving to move'. Motivation is when we feel we want to, or need to, behave in a certain way and sustain it. It is a driving force. However, what motivates any of us is not constant. A wide range of events and factors can change what motivates us. Furthermore, our different personalities and drivers affect how we respond to events. The fact that there is a changing set of circumstances makes it very important that you have some understanding of the principles of motivation so that you enhance the chances of your team members feeling motivated and positive and wanting to do even more.

Needs-based motivation

The idea behind this approach is that people are motivated by unsatisfied needs and feel driven to reach a level of satisfaction with that set of needs. One of the most widely used theories was developed by Abraham Maslow. Although it is nearly 70 years since he first presented the concept, it still holds true today and is used in many disciplines in addition to leadership (e.g. marketing and sales). His original premise was that there is a hierarchy of five levels of need. (Some have broken this down to seven or eight levels, but we will keep to the original idea.) These are shown in Figure 8.1 opposite.

The reason for referring to it as a hierarchy is not that it is 'better' to have your needs at a higher level, it is that there is an ascending order where the lower level has to be reasonably satisfied before the next one comes into focus. For example, if the basic or physiology level is not satisfied because you cannot afford to buy food or pay for heating, you are not too bothered about how you get on with your team colleagues (belonging), or achieving the latest objectives you have been given (ego and esteem).

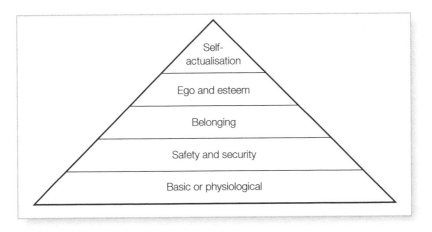

figure 8.1   **Maslow's Hierarchy of Needs**

Source: Figure from Maslow, A., 'A theory of human motivation', *Psychological Review*, 50, pp.370–96 (American Psychological Association, 1943)

The core components of each need level are:

Basic or physiological: air, food, water, heat, shelter, sleep.

Safety and security: job security, health, family, stability, protection (insurance, etc.).

Belonging: family, affection, acceptance, friendships, team colleagues, social groups.

Ego and esteem: achievement, self-esteem, recognition of others, status.

Self-actualisation: feeling of fulfilling potential, stimulation, personal growth, creativity, freedom of thinking.

As a leader you need to know your team members well enough to have a reasonable idea of which level is not being satisfied for them at present. This is where they can be motivated. Maslow stated that you should pay attention to satisfying the lower levels before moving up. (When the team is in 'forming' or 'storming' they need you to use the S1 or telling style from Situational Leadership. Giving clear direction and tasks and then checking will help to meet the safety and security need which has to be satisfied before belonging is important.) Do remember, though, that not everyone has the same needs at the same time. As people move up the pyramid, the needs become more psychological and arguably provide a greater degree of satisfaction.

Do be aware that unmet needs will lead to demotivation. This will become apparent in people's behaviour which can range from apathy to negativity. Another point to recognise is that we can go back down the hierarchy. If someone was at level 4, ego and esteem, but is struggling to pay their rent or mortgage, or there are rumours of redundancies, then the lower levels will be where their needs are – and need to be met.

To use Maslow's hierarchy ask:

Where do I think you really are?

Where do you want to be?

Two factor theory

The most well-known work for this approach was produced by Frederick Herzberg in *The Motivation to Work*.[1] He asked many people in different jobs at different levels two questions:

What factors lead you to experience extreme dissatisfaction with your job?

What factors lead you to experience extreme satisfaction with your job?

He then collated these and found that the following were the main factors in each category:

Leading to satisfaction	*Leading to dissatisfaction*
Achievement	*Company policy*
Recognition	*Supervision*
Work itself	*Relationship with boss*
Responsibility	*Work conditions*
Advancement	*Salary*
Growth	*Relationship with peers*
	Security

He called the factors which caused positive satisfaction 'motivators' and those which offered no satisfaction and led to demotivation if not present 'hygiene'.

	Present	*Absent*
Motivators	Satisfaction	No satisfaction
Hygiene	No dissatisfaction	Dissatisfaction

When the motivators are present, and part of the job and the way the leader treats their team, people will get satisfaction. If these are not present, people will not feel satisfaction and may be a bit negative, but it is more a slight feeling of discontent, or they are apathetic. The hygiene factors are called this because, as in the medical context, when things are hygienic the environment prevents disease or illness – it does not cure it. If the hygiene factors are addressed there might be a slight, short-term motivation but the more likely situation is that there is no dissatisfaction, it is a more neutral feeling. If the hygiene factors are absent, or ignored, there will be a sense of dissatisfaction. This can lead to people actively complaining and moaning to each other and becoming even more demotivated.

If you look at the two lists of factors there is a significant difference between them. Those which lead to satisfaction are all 'intrinsic', i.e. come from within the individual, and those which lead to dissatisfaction are 'extrinsic', i.e. are external. When you look at the lists, you can see that the hygiene side mostly ties in with the lower three levels in Maslow's hierarchy and the motivators match the top two levels. As a leader you have a limited amount of influence on the individuals' acceptance and response to the intrinsic factors. You can provide the climate and opportunity for the individual to respond to them, but you cannot make someone actually do this and feel motivated. That is down to them. Put simply, if you recognise that the main motivators and drivers are intrinsic you cannot make someone feel motivated. They have to make that decision. What you can do is work really hard at keeping things clean, disinfected and hygienic to reduce the dissatisfaction. Although you cannot control all aspects of these factors, how you support your team, handle company policy and manage your team relationships will help towards this. The reality is that the role of many leaders is one where they end up demotivating their teams because they fail to pay attention to these aspects. The important thing is to quietly work at looking after the hygiene and freeing up your people to enjoy the motivators. Create the climate for them to be motivated.

The three elements of intrinsic motivation

Daniel Pink, in *Drive: The Surprising Truth About What Motivates Us*, suggested that there are three elements of internal motivation, which he calls 'autonomy', 'mastery' and 'purpose'.[2] These intrinsic elements might seem to be much common sense, but many leaders forget how internal our motivational drivers are. Pink's ideas help to identify why extrinsic factors have only short-term benefits if any. They also tie in with Herzberg's conclusions.

Autonomy

This is something of a challenge for many managers and leaders to recognise and to allow. Pink suggests that our default setting is to be autonomous and self-directed. For this to happen people need freedom over what they do, when they do it, who they do it with and how they do it. This is an idealised description because there is a fine line between autonomy, as expressed by Pink, and anarchy! However, as leaders, think about how much scope you have to give team members more freedom and flexibility in these areas. It can pay dividends if you can be less directive and more empowering.

Mastery

Pink believes that people need to be engaged in their work and it is this which leads to mastery. If we are interested in something we will want to become better at it. We want to grow and stretch ourselves and our skills. He suggests that there are three parts to mastery. These relate to the 'mind set' where we believe we can continue to improve, the 'stretch' which needs us to put in the effort and practice, and the fact it is 'progressive' because you cannot actually achieve full mastery, you can always do something better.

Purpose

Although they may not be able to articulate it, most people have a sense of purpose and want to feel they are working towards it. The clearer our sense of purpose, almost like our personal vision, the more we can direct our energies into activities which lead towards it.

These three ideas may explain why many organisations and leaders do not get the most out of their people. They rely too heavily on the extrinsic factors to get people to be motivated. More power is produced when a person wants something they themselves have decided to go for.

Equity theory

In an article in *Advances in Experimental Social Psychology*, J. Stacey Adams introduced a concept which brought together a number of the ideas about motivation in what he called the Equity Theory.[3] It was very different because at its core is the idea that it is based on the perception of fairness and we use comparison to decide on this. We make decisions about the balance between our *inputs* and our *outputs* depending on how fair we perceive the ratio between them to be, especially when compared with others who we consider to be similar.

Inputs are what we give or put into our work which covers a wide range of our skills, energies and attitudes. Outputs are everything we take out or are offered in return and include a lot more than just money.

INPUTS	EQUITY	OUTPUTS
	Depends on comparison of own ratio of input/output with ratios of 'referent' others.	
Inputs are typically: work effort, loyalty, commitment, using skills, adaptability, flexibility, tolerance, determination, heart and soul, enthusiasm, trust in our boss and superiors, support of colleagues and team, personal sacrifice, commitment, etc.	People need to feel that there is a fair balance between inputs and outputs. Fairness is measured by comparing one's own balance or ratio between inputs and outputs with the ratio enjoyed or endured by relevant ('referent') others.	Outputs are what you get from your job. A combination of all financial rewards – salary, expenses, benefits, pension arrangements, bonus and commission – plus intangibles – recognition, reputation, praise and thanks, interest, responsibility, stimulus, travel, training, development, sense of achievement and advancement, promotion, etc.

If people feel that inputs are *fairly* rewarded by outputs (fairness being subjective and perceived against local and market norms and other references, possibly internal to the organisation), then generally they are happier about work and more motivated to continue inputting at the same or a higher level.

Should we feel that the ratio of inputs to outputs is less fair than the ratio enjoyed by referent others, then we become demotivated. For most people the level of demotivation is proportional to the perceived difference with other people or inequity. However, for some people the slightest indication of a negative disparity will trigger feelings of disappointment and injustice, resulting in demotivation. This can lead to reduced effort, internal and external muttering and moaning, or becoming unco-operative. If they cannot adjust the balance by improving their outputs scale they may look for another job.

Equity theory has several implications for leaders:

- People measure the totals of their inputs and outcomes according to their own situation and priorities. For example, a working mother may accept a lower salary in return for more flexible working hours.

- People decide on equity according to their personal values in relation to inputs and outcomes. Two people of equal experience and qualification doing the same role for the same salary may have different perceptions of the fairness of the deal.

- Although it may be understood and acceptable for more senior managers and directors to receive higher salaries and packages, there are limits to the balance of the scales of equity. People can find excessive executive pay demotivating.

- Team members' perceptions of the inputs and outcomes they achieve and those of others may be incorrect. As a leader you may need to step in and clear these up and influence these perceptions effectively.

- A person who believes they are over-compensated may increase effort. However, it may be that they develop a sense of superiority and actually decrease efforts.

Developing your team

A quality of good leaders is their ability to bring the best out of their people by a variety of means. One of the most effective ways of achieving this is to look for opportunities to coach their team members. Some manage to do this without thinking about it, or having no understanding of the process. They naturally encourage, push and support their team members without having labels for what they are doing. Some know they should do it but think it will be really difficult and requires a lot of training before they can begin – and they don't have time for it. The result is they do nothing. Others think developing people in the organisation should be done by the HR or training department who provide courses.

Coaching does not have to be complex or difficult. It is a skill which can be learned and taken to a high level with various qualifications. However, you do not need to go through these steps in order to be effective as a coach for your team. Begin with a willingness to start coaching your people, use good communication skills and acquire some understanding of coaching models and you will be able to do a productive job in developing your team members.

A core competence for your role as a leader is developing others. The qualities of effective developers are listed below and those of less effective developers are shown too. They provide a useful checklist for your attitudes and behaviours.

EFFECTIVE DEVELOPER	INEFFECTIVE DEVELOPER
Operates as a part-time trainer	Overlooks development aspect of job
Creates a positive climate for learning	Fails to create a conducive climate for learning within team
Understands the development needs of team members	Unaware of development needs of team
Stretches team members through objectives, delegation and projects	Does not stretch team members
Uses reviews regularly and constructively	Uses reviews infrequently and ineffectively
Knows strengths and weaknesses of team members	Does not know or clarify strengths and weaknesses of team members
Believes in the potential of people to develop	Does not believe potential of people or ignores it
Gives feedback skilfully and constructively	Unskilled at giving feedback
Looks for work opportunities for development of people	Fails to use development opportunities in the workplace, thinks it is HR's job

If asked, could you explain or define coaching? Probably not. First, let me clear up one common misconception. Coaching is *not* instructing or training another.

Coaching is working with others to encourage them to grow and develop. It involves supporting and challenging others to help them move forward.

It can be defined as: *The art of facilitating the performance, learning and development of another.* It is about using day-to-day events and work as learning experiences. This is a key aspect of good coaching. It is something which requires you, as the leader, to be able to observe what your team members are doing as part of their day-to-day work – and how they are doing it. This provides you with real time and real life opportunities to help your team. (Unlike a manager at a client of mine, who manages a 'team' of sales people. At a recent workshop one of his team said she would send him a plan for him to read through. When I suggested it would be more effective to share and discuss it with him, she agreed. However, in five months, he had never spent any time out with her in the field or with customers. How is he supposed to know her skills and performance with customers just by sitting behind his desk?)

The good leader as a coach has the attitude and belief that others can continue to develop and improve and that they want to when given the right encouragement and help. You have to start with this attitude. It is important that you approach any coaching interaction by creating an environment where the person being coached feels safe and secure. If they are going to be happy to be challenged and stretched they need to feel this first and to believe you will support them. To achieve this, you need to build a rapport with them.

Many times coaching will be something which requires you to sit down and have a reasonable length discussion. Occasionally, it can be a brief conversation almost in passing. Each approach has value in supporting the on-going development of your team.

The first step to take is paying attention to what your team members are doing and how. From this you can identify some specific areas where you think they could improve. This then gives you the chance to approach the person and start to have a discussion about the 'performance gap' (see Figure 8.2). This is critical if the person is going to be open to coaching. You need to be specific about the current performance you saw. The challenge can be in getting agreement about the desired level. If the other person does not agree that this is as high as you think, consider negotiating a reasonable level that they can aim for. Once they reach this, you can look to move on still higher.

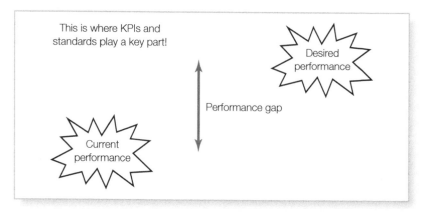

This is where KPIs and standards play a key part!

Desired performance

Performance gap

Current performance

figure 8.2 Establishing the performance gap

How to coach

You need to remember the core communication skills about expressing yourself clearly and listening. There is no particular science or skill set required if you are using effective communication and interpersonal skills. The only one we have not addressed yet is how to give effective feedback. This is important in many aspects of your leadership, not just coaching.

1   Definition of feedback

Any communication, verbal or non-verbal, which offers a person some information about how they affect others.

2   Importance of feedback

Feedback has a fundamental role to play in terms of:

Awareness: helping people become more aware of themselves and their impact on others.

Choices: helping people increase their repertoire of behaviours and relate to others.

Decisions: helping people to reinforce or question their decisions.

In other words, feedback helps people clarify and explore their behaviours and to identify additional ways of managing them.

Guidelines on giving feedback:

▪ Make sure the person you are giving feedback to wants to receive it. This is a process between consenting adults, not a battle.

▪ Be specific, quote examples, say what you saw or heard, use evidence, state what you thought the result was.

▪ Give at least as much 'positive' feedback as 'could have done better'.

▪ Don't criticise people for what they cannot help; give feedback on performance or behaviour, not personality.

▪ Be timely. Don't wait for a month, or for the annual appraisal – it's too late by then.

▪ Make sure that the environment is right

▪ Do not overload with feedback, watch for the signs.

Key points to consider for making feedback effective:

1   Focus on what you see   *not on what you believe*
2   Focus on behaviour   *not on personality*
3   Keep it neutral   *don't make judgements*
4   Use it to inform   *not to advise*
5   Make it supportive   *rather than threatening*
6   Keep it simple   *don't overdo it*
7   If you give it   *you have to be able to take it*

Having given feedback and established the performance gap, you can start coaching. This could be through simple questioning. However, there are many slightly more structured or formal approaches you can use which are helpful.

When you have spotted something in the day-to-day work situation, a really useful model is ROAR. Its major benefit is that it has a degree of immediacy about what is happening and what you want to make happen. It will then encourage the other person to begin taking immediate steps – and quickly lead to improvements.

The stages are:

RIGHT NOW (what is happening – what you saw)

OPTIONS (what options or choices might be effective in improving or correcting the situation)

ACTION (agreeing on the specific actions the individual will take – and creating an action plan)

REVIEW (considering how things went, what they achieved and learned – and agreeing the next steps)

If you go to Chapter 10 there is more detail about this model and some examples of questions you can use for each stage.

Where the area for coaching might be more medium or long term and involve more change from the individual, then GROW might be more effective.

GOALS – what does the person want to achieve? When by?

REALITY – what is happening at present? Where are they now? What might stop them?

OPTIONS – what ideas do they have for achieving the goal? Who else could help?

WILL – how committed are they to working on this? What support do they need?

(More detail appears in Chapter 10.)

The key skill you need to use with either of these is listening and questioning. It is not your role to tell the other person what to do, nor do you have to offer suggestions unless they are really stuck. Another element to skilful coaching is believing that the team member can work out their own way of dealing with their situation and your task is to facilitate them in doing so. It might take some time for them to think about their answers and to arrive at their conclusions, but the more you practise the better you all become at the process.

The other coaching approach is the short and sharp option. This is very useful at review time, or when someone has just completed a particular task or activity.

Give feedback on what you observed. Ask:

> How did you think that went?
>
> What went well?
>
> What will you do differently if doing it again?
>
> What did you learn from it?

Coaching does not have to be complicated, nor need you fear doing it. Look for opportunities to coach and you will keep developing your team. This contributes to their motivation in many ways and also improves their perception of you. When they become accustomed to the coaching climate and process, they will enjoy it and appreciate your role in it. By developing the team members to achieve their potential, and even extend it, you will be building the talent within the team and for the organisation.

Recognising and rewarding achievement

In the 'Motivation' section we covered the difference between intrinsic and extrinsic factors and their part in motivating people. The extrinsic ones have less impact on long-term satisfaction and motivation and this is important to remember when looking for ideas to recognise and reward achievement and performance. At the same time, do not ignore some extrinsic elements.

When you think about all of the theories of motivation they all involve recognition or reward in one way or another. There are a number of options you can consider using to achieve this depending on the circumstances of the achievement, the individual's drivers and your organisation's policy.

Recognition

One of the quickest ways to start disillusioning teams and team members is to set objectives and then ignore people when they achieve them. (Going back to the ABCs in Chapter 6 and using the 'no response' option – see p.81.) Taking the view that 'they are paid to do that' might be true but is not very productive or helpful. The situation can be made even worse if the leader starts on the 'OK, that wasn't bad – *but* . . .' attitude. As human beings we all need some degree of acknowledgement and recognition, some more than others. No one likes being ignored, especially when they know they have achieved or completed something.

To make recognition valuable, give it for something specific not just as a generalised statement. When someone has completed a task well, or handled a situation well, give the praise and acknowledgement promptly (and publicly). Also, be specific about what the recognition is for. This makes it more valuable and reinforces the behaviour behind it. Recognition can be given in my ways and spread around the organisation too. Apart from delivering it personally in a face-to-face situation it can be delivered at meetings in front of colleagues and also to the team if that is relevant. Giving recognition through the written word, whether by e-mail or a letter, can have even more impact, especially if copying other people to spread the word.

Case study

Several years ago I was interviewing sales people and account managers to fill a vacancy for a client. One of the applicants had worked for a major Japanese company and while with them had a massive success with one of his customers, knocking out their number one competitor. The sale earned him a very large commission (it was equivalent to about half of his year's quota).

When I asked him what he really enjoyed and remembered about this, he told me that while the money was helpful, and paid off a good piece of his mortgage, the thing he really felt good about was receiving a hand-written note from the president of the company in Japan. As he said, the money was nice but spent, the note he still had and treasured. As far as he knew, at the time, he was the only employee of the organisation in the UK who had ever received a personal note from the president.

As leaders we should never underestimate the power of recognition. Where it is appropriate you might get managers up the line to deliver some form of recognition to your team members. It does not undermine yours, it reinforces it.

You might have seen examples of 'Employee of the Month' awards in hotels and restaurants or other environments. This is another form of recognition which can work, provided it is given for genuine reasons and for really good performance. Finding ways of making the recognition more visible to more people can be another good option. Not everyone will be driven to get their picture or name in lights, but it is still a way of showing that you have recognised and acknowledged what someone has done. Other visible forms of recognition can be done through different forms of 'status'. This can range from badges or broaches, ties or scarves to cars or job titles.

Recognition is something you and the organisation can give. Failing to do so can lead to some level of disillusionment, but when you do give it you cannot make someone accept it and feel good and motivated. Although the delivery is extrinsic, and some of the examples above are definitely in that category, the response has to be intrinsic. How it is handled by the individual does depend on their own personality, the organisational culture and the broader local culture.

Rewarding

When talking about rewarding achievement many people only think about money. While this is frequently the case, and even the default option in many places, it is not the only choice. If you have the opportunity to give bonuses or similar based on performance, that is not to be derided. Having said this, the motivational impact from the bonus is tied in to the fact it is a recognition of the performance rather than the money itself. At times, the money against performance is meeting the ego and esteem need if it is going to enable the recipient to buy their new, bigger car, etc. Other ways of rewarding performance can be giving additional time off, freedom about ways of working, additional responsibility, promotion, sending on conferences or external events and incentive trips, or even share option schemes or similar ideas around some type of involvement with owning a small piece of the business. The list is limited by the scope you have within your organisation.

The reality with a number of these options for recognising and rewarding achievement is that many are part of the 'carrot' end of the carrot and stick approach to motivation. The more intrinsic your choices the better, partly because when we start offering 'carrots' people can begin to take them as an expectation, so we need to give larger 'carrots', especially the extrinsic ones.

When you have team members who are growing in their roles and performing really well, a very powerful way of motivating them is to look for opportunities to develop them through additional responsibility and delegation and putting them forward for promotion where possible. Although it might seem frustrating to grow your people to then lose them to promotion, it should do the opposite. If you do not do it, your better people will look to leave anyway. Once it is recognised that you have a team environment where people can develop and grow and be promoted your reputation as a leader will be stronger. Your team will become an attractive place to be and you will find good quality people want to be a part of it. You can think about their moving onwards and upwards as a sign that you are doing a great job as a leader and getting more from your people.

Summary

- People are your main resource, so focus on how to keep getting more from them. They deliver the performance you are judged on.

- Motivation is mainly driven by intrinsic, or internal, factors. Whether these are seen as positive is the individual's choice. You cannot make someone feel good or respond to these factors.

- There is no one way of motivating your team, so understand the principles within the different theories and find those which you are comfortable with and can apply with your team.

- Avoid being a demotivator for your team – which is the unintended function of many leaders!

- See yourself as a developer. This helps you lift the capability and performance of your team members and it supports motivation too.

- Be willing to make mistakes as you practise coaching, you will improve. It is better to coach and make mistakes in the process than not do any coaching.

- When people achieve things, look to give the most appropriate recognition or reward for them. Choose whatever will work best for them, not for you.

References

[1] Frederick Herzberg, *The Motivation to Work*, John Wiley and Sons, 1959.

[2] Daniel Pink, *Drive: The Surprising Truth About What Motivates Us*, Penguin, 2009.

[3] J. Stacey Adams, 'Inequity in social exchange', *Advances in Experimnetal Social Psychology*, 1965.

Handling challenges within the team

Leading successful teams is not always plain sailing. It would be very pleasant and easy if this was the case. However, at any stage of its development a team can provide the leader with a number of challenges. These can be any of the following: conflict; lack of commitment to the task or objectives; communication breakdowns; or personality clashes. While not ideal, these need not be harmful or damaging if you are able to handle them in the right way. The thing to avoid is doing nothing and hoping the problem will go away. It is extremely unlikely to do so and it is more probably going to fester and get worse, which will have a damaging effect on performance. You need to take control and act to address the issue and find ways of resolving it with the team members who are involved. This will not always prove easy to accomplish. It requires a degree of courage and determination from you, which is part of strong leadership. In this chapter I will give you some suggestions for tackling each of these challenges.

In Chapter 2, we introduced you to the group dynamics process. The initial 'forming' stage presents its own challenges because you need to provide most of the direction and it takes time to get the team to engage with the objectives, standards, etc. and to commit to them. As they move into the 'storming' stage you will encounter more of the challenges listed above. These do need to be dealt with appropriately so that the team can progress to 'norming' and 'performing'. When the team is operating at these levels it is easy to think that they should be beyond the challenges. This is not necessarily the case. There can still be conflict, personality clashes and various challenges. They need to be addressed and they may need you to intervene to help resolve things positively. In many instances, if the team are really at the upper levels, these situations might arise and they will deal with them amongst themselves in a constructive way.

If there are no challenges or disagreements it does not mean that everything is really going well. There is a risk that the team members are more concerned with getting along together and focusing on the harmony of the group rather than the results they need to achieve. This leads to 'groupthink'. In many respects this can be the most harmful and tricky of all of the challenges the leader might face. It is easy to feel that things are going well because there is no obvious problem or conflict and to assume that it means the team is functioning effectively.

If you think that your team is slipping towards groupthink you need to take action to prevent it. Consider it as another challenge within the team and don't think it is a pleasant, harmonious state. It will limit the team's potential performance. The term was originally introduced by William H. Whyte Jnr in an article in *Fortune* magazine in 1952.[1] More research and studying of the specific behaviours was carried out by Irving Janis and initially written up in *Psychology Today* in 1971.[2] This, and further work since then, reinforces how it prevents teams achieving what they are capable of.

Dealing with groupthink

The dangers of groupthink can be illustrated in a variety of historical events and business setbacks or failures. One example is how Swissair went from being known as 'The Flying Bank' to collapsing in the early 2000s. The group thought they were invulnerable because of their consistent financial success and were not adapting to market forces. They had reduced the size of the board, removing members with aviation industry knowledge. The board members lacked specific expertise in the industry and had similar backgrounds combined with their values. A perfect situation for encouraging conformity of thinking. There were no challenging voices or different inputs to make them think about alternative strategies or external threats.

Groupthink is the way of thinking that happens when the desire for harmony in a team overrides people's willingness to speak up to offer different ideas or alternatives to the way they do things. Team members aim to minimise the risk of conflict and reach a consensus decision without challenge or critical evaluation of alternative ideas or viewpoints.

Typical symptoms of groupthink are as follows:

> Thinking the team or group is so strong it will not make mistakes.
>
> The team belief is so powerful they feel that choices they will make will be good for everyone.
>
> The team do not take any notice of anyone who might challenge them and dismiss their input.
>
> Internal pressures to conform. Team members are considered disloyal or misguided if they challenge the norm or consensus. Silence is considered to be the same as agreement.

Any combination of these symptoms will limit the quality of decision making and outputs.

You can take steps to prevent groupthink from becoming a standard behaviour within your team.

Based on the research of Janis you can introduce the following:

1   Encourage everyone to understand their preferred team roles (from Chapter 3) and to use these when working together. Also, recognise and value the differences between the roles, why they are needed and how each contributes to effective performance.

2   Assign each member the function of 'critical evaluator'. This allows each member to freely air objections and doubts. Those who have the 'monitor evaluator' as a preferred team role will do this naturally.

3   Senior managers or more experienced team members should avoid expressing opinions when assigning tasks to the team and allow them to express their thoughts about the task.

4   All effective alternatives to any problem or challenge should be encouraged and examined.

5   Each team member should share or discuss the team's ideas with trusted people outside of the team.

6   It can be very constructive to invite outside experts into meetings. Team members should be encouraged to discuss with and question the outside expert.

7   At least one group member should be assigned the role of devil's advocate. This should be a different person for each meeting so that everyone becomes more comfortable with challenging ideas and doing so in a constructive manner. Having said this, do not force the role on someone who is naturally quiet and reserved unless they are comfortable with assuming it.

Having a team where people can get along and enjoy each other's company can be a good thing for you as a leader. However, they do need to be comfortable with disagreeing with each other and putting forward their own ideas. This tells you that they are working well and not slipping into 'groupthink' with all of its risks for performance.

Handling conflict constructively

What do you think about when you hear the word conflict? I would imagine you do not view it as a positive word or think of conflict situations as good. Your team members probably feel the same. Many of us react to potential or actual conflict situations by trying to avoid them, especially if we have had an unpleasant experience before. We all have a preferred style when reacting to conflict. The most widely used model for assessing these was developed by Kenneth Thomas and Ralph Kilman in 1974. It considers our response on two axes, the degree of co-operativeness (wishing to work or get along with, or to consider the other person and their needs or goals) and the amount of assertiveness we use (standing our own ground, wanting to make our point or get our own way, the focus on our own needs or goals). Using these they identified five possible styles for responding to conflict, as shown in Figure 9.1.

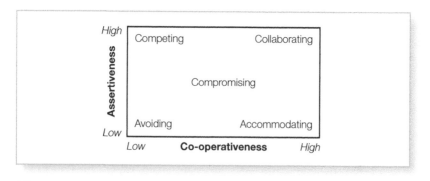

figure 9.1   **The five styles**

Competing is assertive and unco-operative – an individual pursues their own concerns at the other person's expense. This is a power-oriented mode, in which the person uses whatever power seems appropriate to achieve or win their own position – whether using their ability to argue, their position or power for economic sanctions. Competing might mean 'standing up for your rights', defending a position which you believe is correct or simply trying to win. Some people who use this too much could be seen as aggressive or domineering and closed minded because they do not consider anyone else's position.

Accommodating is unassertive and co-operative – the opposite of competing. When accommodating, an individual neglects their own concerns to satisfy the concerns of the other person; there is an element of self-sacrifice in this mode. Accommodating might take the form of selfless generosity, obeying another person's order when one would prefer not to or yielding to another's point of view. There are times when it can be useful to use this style such as when a senior person is stating something and it is easier to go along with them or when the issue is not that important to you and you decide to let it go.

Avoiding is unassertive and unco-operative – the individual does not immediately pursue their own concerns or those of the other person. They do not address the conflict. Avoiding might take the form of diplomatically side-stepping an issue, postponing an issue until a better time or simply withdrawing from a threatening situation. Another form of avoiding that some people use is trying to change the subject or introducing humour hoping it will distract from the issue.

Collaborating is both assertive and co-operative – the opposite of avoiding. Collaborating involves an attempt to work with the other person to find a solution which fully satisfies the concerns of both. It means digging into an issue to identify the underlying concerns of the two parties to find alternatives which meet both sets of concerns. Collaborating between two parties might take the form of exploring a disagreement to learn from each other's insights, or confronting and trying to find a creative solution to an interpersonal problem. It does require both parties to work towards an agreed end and needs a willingness to be open to considering different options provided they can lead towards the desired outcome.

Compromising is intermediate in both assertiveness and co-operativeness. The objective is to find some expedient, mutually acceptable solution which partially satisfies both parties. It falls on a middle ground between competing and accommodating. Compromising gives up more than competing but less than accommodating. Likewise, it addresses an issue more directly than avoiding, but doesn't explore it in as much depth as collaborating. Compromising might mean splitting the difference, exchanging concessions or seeking a quick middle-ground position. It can be a 'quick-fix' solution that each can accept without being totally happy with the outcome. It is useful for dealing with issues which are not too complex or are not critical to the working of the team.

What is conflict? I like this definition: 'A process which begins when one party perceives that the other has frustrated, or is about to frustrate, some concern of theirs.' 'This makes the point that what we often fear about conflict, the risk of the fight or battle, is actually the end of the process. It usually starts off as a small level of frustration or disagreement and escalates because it is not addressed early.

Conflict can be a negative and, unfortunately, this is the way which most people think about it (see Figure 9.2). It leads to win–lose decision making, the quality of relationships deteriorates and can lead to people actively avoiding each other and only interacting when they have to. If this is the way conflict is being addressed within the team or between team members the danger is that things will get worse and worse. This can lead to increasing levels of demotivation for those involved and even for other team members. It will certainly have a negative impact on communication, relationships and performance.

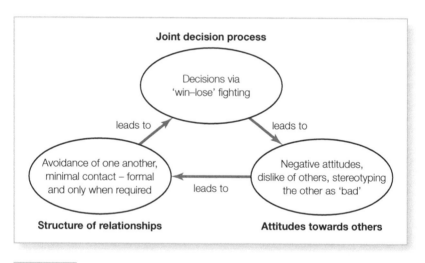

figure 9.2 Negative conflict

We often forget that conflict, when handled properly, can be positive (see Figure 9.3). If the team members know how to address their differences and disagreements in a constructive manner, they can be more collaborative in arriving at decisions. This gives them a very different attitude towards each other and leads to more positive relationships. You need to know how to help your team members to move towards this way of dealing with disagreements and help them feel confident about confronting situations rather than avoiding them. Doing this does not mean that the issue will go away. It is resolved by working it out. At the same time you do not want the team slipping into 'group-think' – they have to air their opinions and any disagreements.

As the leader you may have to handle conflict situations which arise between you and someone else or to be the facilitator where the differences are between team members. Using a structured approach can help you to address the conflict in a constructive and positive way, feeling more confident and calm about doing so.

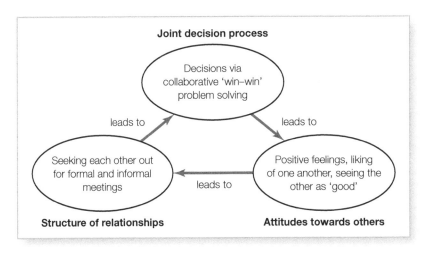

figure 9.4   Positive conflict

A step-by-step approach to addressing conflict

This process works well whether the issue is between you and another or if you are acting as the mediator between two or more people. In the latter case, it might help to explain the overall process first, or at least summarise the aim of each step.

1   **Present the issue clearly and assertively, using 'I' statements and ask for the other party's help.**

Using 'I' statements ensures your 'ownership' of your position. 'You' statements are likely to be seen as attacking – and produce a defensive response. Aim to present the issue in positive language, i.e. what you want to achieve rather than what you do not want. Focusing on positives encourages a different way of thinking. Too much emphasis on what you do not want can lead to defensiveness from one or both sides.

An effective 'I' statement concludes with a request for co-operation and help. 'Can we agree to work together on this? I really need your help.' Or, 'I would appreciate your thoughts on how we can resolve this.' Most people will want to co-operate and help solve a problem when the issue is presented asking for assistance, rather than as an accusation or a threat. Each needs to be able to state their position without interruption.

2 **Clarify and define the issue.**

Some conflicts are caused by differences in perception rather than facts. 'Here's how I see the problem. What do you think?' This continues until each side has stated how they view the issue. The aim is to reach some agreement or understanding of the issue or problem.

3 **Get the other person's position.**

Ask the other party how they are affected by the problem and to state their position. Listen and acknowledge their position.

4 **Give your point of view.**

Use 'I' statements and assertiveness skills to put your point across. If necessary ask for their understanding of your position, 'How does my position seem to you?'

5 **Jointly develop an outcome about which you can both agree – use the 'Conflict Integration Strategy' (see Figure 9.4).**

Work through the process and keep going until you find a common aim.

6 **Generate alternatives.**

Without prejudging – each side can either write down their preferred outcome and at least three alternatives or you can do this jointly in discussion.

7 **Jointly choose one alternative as a possible solution.**

Consider the alternatives (and remain open to others). Review and discuss until you establish one about which you can both agree – even if only provisionally. State it in writing – and identify specific actions to take to implement it – with a plan.

8   Jointly agree on how each side will know if the solution is working.

What evidence will there be for each side? Develop specific criteria each can use to assess this.

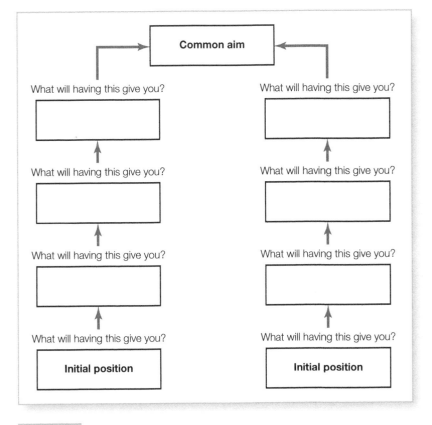

figure 9.4   **Conflict Integration Strategy**

This approach to handling conflict is flexible. You can use it on your own before meeting with the other party or leave it until you are together. It has the added benefit that you can make it visual by writing each step as you go through it, which keeps the attention on the discussion and process rather than the individuals. (Also useful if you are involving several team members.)

Be clear about defining the current situation or 'initial position'. Once this is done ask the question, 'What will having this give you?' You get an answer (which is almost certainly moving to a bigger picture level of thinking) and use the same question and get another answer. Stop after three or four answers, being ready to come back to the last response if you need to. Now put yourself in the other person's shoes and look at things from their point of view and whatever their initial position appears to be. Work through the steps in the same way and see where you have reached after three or four levels. Frequently, you will have reached a situation which offers common ground or a common outcome. You can now talk with the other person and possibly shortcut the conversation by suggesting what you think is the common outcome. This becomes the starting point for resolving the conflict.

If doing this face to face without having worked through it yourself, you can approach it in a couple of ways. Either, explain the process (possibly showing them the diagram), how it works and what you want it to achieve. Alternatively, do it conversationally by asking them to start by stating their position and asking them the questions. Then share your position and go step by step and look for the common ground. Once reached, get clear agreement that both parties want to achieve this. From here, the conversation can focus on how they can each work towards it and what the benefits will be for all concerned, directly and indirectly.

Tackling lack of commitment

Within a team you will often find different levels of commitment to tasks or objectives. Many of the reasons for this are covered in the previous chapter, where we looked at a number of elements of motivation and what might lead to demotivation. You need to have some understanding of the personalities of your team. Just because someone is not acting enthusiastically does not mean that they are lacking commitment or that they are demotivated. Some may be quieter and it is harder to tell whether they are engaged. However, do not presume that is the case.

You can identify a lack of commitment in several ways. It could be overt where people are disagreeing with what you are asking or just not doing what is required. More subtly, they may appear to go along with what is needed and do it to some extent, but not particularly well or enthusiastically. You might spot this when you see small groups getting together and sense that they are muttering about what is being asked of them and generally acting negatively. (This might be more apparent if the team are in the 'storming' phase.)

Many leaders allow this type of challenge to grow and become a bigger issue than it needs to be. They either hope it will suddenly turn round or just evaporate. This is unlikely, because lack of commitment will impact on the performance levels before long. You are then caught in the position of having to deal with this and raise the issue with the team or individuals. Hopefully, you have introduced the right monitoring and control processes (as suggested in Chapter 6) which give you a clear basis against which to raise your concerns. However, this will not necessarily encourage commitment and could even lead to more demotivation, especially if they have not bought in to the controls.

You need to be in tune with your team members and pay attention to their reaction when you have asked them to carry out any particular tasks or set objectives. Even if you are doing this in discussion with them do not think they are committed if you get tacit acceptance. There is a risk that this might slip away once they have left you to a neutral reaction at best or towards a lack of commitment. You need to be sure to get full agreement, not just acceptance. Pay attention to the non-verbal signals they give and do not just go along with the words. Check by asking them for their initial actions to get started on the task. What will they do about any potential barriers or problems?

When you suspect a real lack of commitment, whether from the team as a whole or from a group or an individual, you need to act quickly. The longer you allow the situation to go on the probability is that the level of demotivation will be even greater and the performance will be even further adrift from what is required. This will make dealing with it even harder. In a similar vein to coaching and giving feedback, you need to make sure you have specific examples of behaviour or performance to use when starting to address the issue. Gather your evidence from wherever you can.

The most effective way to deal with this, and some of the other challenges which we cover later, is to be direct and assertive. You need to confront the people and issues concerned. Although you may feel uncomfortable or nervous about this approach, it is what many people would describe as part of good leadership. Being strong and decisive when required is important for your credibility, particularly when there are potential problems within the team.

Choose the right environment for the meeting and discussion.

Be clear and direct, stating what you have observed, how and why you feel this shows a lack of commitment.

Be factual and keep your voice calm, avoiding any form of accusation. (It is fine to say how it makes you feel, 'When this happens... I feel...')

State how you would like people to be behaving.

Ask what is stopping them doing so, why they are not committed.

What needs to be different for them to feel commitment? (Be open to being flexible in your requirement or approach providing the outcome is what you need to achieve and the KPIs or standards are still met.)

How can we all work together to maintain the commitment? How can we spot any slippage and act to correct it early?

Handling communication breakdowns

Your team can have communication breakdowns internally and externally and neither is helpful to their performance or development. Addressing these will improve relationships within the team, and those they deal with outside, and will improve the efficiency and effectiveness of their work. Breakdowns lead to poor information flow or exchange, misunderstandings and distrust, amongst many other problems.

When you recognise that there is an issue with communication between team members, or some of them and you, act to correct it. Time is of the essence; the longer the problem goes on the worse things will become between the people involved. This type of problem will often be an underlying cause for later conflict. It is better to deal with it at this stage. The relatively good news is that issues in this area are usually less contentious to raise with your team members than some of the other challenges.

Handling these situations requires a similar process to the commitment challenges. Gather specific data or examples so that you are not being subjective when you raise the issue.

Be timely – act as quickly as reasonable after recognising the situation so that it is fresh in people's minds.

Be clear and direct, stating what you have observed and what are the consequences or risks.

Explore the reasons for the breakdown, with a firm 'no blame' rule.

What can everyone do to prevent this happening in the future?

How can we create a culture to support and challenge each other to prevent breakdowns happening?

How can we apply these principles when interacting outside the team?

Dealing with personality clashes

Even when reaching a high-performing level teams can have occasions when some individuals fall out with each other for a variety of reasons. It is not essential that all team members are good friends or get on well together. What is needed is for them to respect their colleagues for their contribution and trust each other to do what is expected. However, there can be times when individuals do struggle to get on or work together and this can build to personality clashes. When these arise within a team they can have a damaging influence on the individuals, their motivation and interaction, and subsequent performance. To make things worse, if the personality clash becomes too bad it can begin to harm the communication within the team and cause others to feel frustrated or to avoid interacting with the feuding people.

You probably think that dealing with this type of challenge is the one you would most like to avoid, or at least defer. That is understandable because we tend to imagine the worst when thinking of intervening and anticipate arguments and anger from those involved. Whether this happens or not you have to step in and resolve the situation. The consequences of personality clashes for the individuals, the team and you are potentially significant and become greater the longer you delay.

The type of team you are leading and the physical location of where people work will dictate how easily you can identify any personality clashes, or spot the early warning signs of them arising. Whatever the circumstances, be prepared to intervene on your earliest suspicions. It is preferable to apologise and admit you might have been wrong rather than wait until it has escalated to the point of individuals not speaking or interacting.

You have choices about how to address issues in this area. Which you select is dependent on the location of the individuals, urgency of the situation, the personalities involved and your own preference. The first option is to talk to each of the individuals involved separately and get their description of the background and situation. The alternative is to bring the people together in a room and let each explain the situation in turn and then move forward. The steps overleaf can be used in either of these options.

1   Act quickly, as soon as you can see or hear a potential problem.

2   Be clear and direct, stating what you have observed and what are the possible consequences for the team performance.

3   Establish some ground rules – e.g. the speaker is to be allowed to continue uninterrupted, each has to listen to the other, comments to be about behaviour not personality, no blaming of the other, voices to stay under control.

4   Each to state why the situation has arisen from their perspective.

5   Each to explore what they could have done differently.

6   What can they do differently in the future to prevent a recurrence?

7   If they suspect the friction is building what can they do to bring it back?

8   Each has to agree to the last two points.

If struggling to move the people forward, consider using the ideas for resolving conflict which we covered earlier in the chapter.

Summary

- Challenges will happen even in the most effective and productive teams.

- Disagreements and different points of view can be useful and constructive in the team, providing they are expressed in the right way, listened to and acknowledged properly.

- Lack of disagreements and everyone going for the easy option of agreeing to all ideas is not helpful. It leads to 'groupthink' and that is not a good behaviour for effective team performance and is just as much of a challenge to the leader as conflict.

- When you see or sense any of the challenges happening within the team, take action. Allowing them to carry on (hoping the problems might go away) is not an option for good leadership. Your team look to you to deal with tricky or tough situations so do what they need to see.

- Early intervention will prevent the problem spreading or having too big an impact on the team and performance.

- It is generally less difficult to deal with the issues in their early stages rather than when they are getting established.

- Any of the challenges covered here can spread like a virus within the team. It is ideal if you can prevent them even starting. Realistically, even in the best performing teams tensions and challenges can occur. The secret is to act to isolate them before they become infectious.

References

[1] William H. Whyte Jnr, 'Groupthink', *Fortune*, March, 1952.

[2] Irving L. Janis, 'Groupthink', *Psychology Today*, 5, November, 1971.

part

3

Reviewing and coaching

10

Pulling it all together

Summary of the benefits of high-performance teams

It is surprisingly difficult to find objective evidence to prove that high-performance teams are more successful or productive in the workplace. Studies have been done with groups on management development programmes, with work teams as part of PhD theses and similar situations. Logically, it could be awkward to evaluate two teams or more in the workplace and compare their performance and assess how they interact as teams. There are examples which can be drawn from within the armed forces, medical teams in operating theatres and aircrews on the flight deck which support the messages carried throughout this book.

Thinking about it logically, a team that shares a common aim, is working towards it using the individuals' qualities and strengths, supports each other, communicates openly and is well led is likely to perform well and better than one lacking some or all of these. If in doubt, watch *The Apprentice* for some fantastic insights on how *not* to lead or work in an effective, high-performing team.

High-performing teams will produce better results for the organisation, usually more efficiently too. They will set an example or provide a role model which others may aspire to copy or join. They will be stimulating and enjoyable places to work, with motivated team members. Those involved with the team, including the leader, will be considered for promotion or development. In short, everyone can benefit.

Some key thoughts for each step

Chapter 1 Facing the challenges of leading your team

Remember, being an effective team leader does not just happen! You need to think about what is required and make sure you spend time working on the important things.

There are some differences between management and leadership, as shown in the table below. However the really effective team leader will balance the two roles appropriately.

	Management	Leadership
What are we setting out to do?	Planning and budgeting – establishing detailed steps and timetables for achieving the results, and then allocating the resources required to make it happen.	Establishing direction – developing a vision for the future, often the distant future, and the strategies for producing the changes to achieve that vision.
How do we encourage our people to deliver the required results?	Organising and staffing – establishing some structure to achieve the plan requirements, staffing, delegating responsibility and authority for carrying out the plan, provide the policies and procedures or systems to monitor progress.	Aligning people – communicating the direction by words and deeds to those whose co-operation may be needed to influence the creation of teams that understand the vision and strategies and want to achieve them.
Making it happen	Controlling and problem solving – monitoring results against the plan, identifying deviations and planning and organising to correct these problems.	Motivating and inspiring – energising people to overcome major political, bureaucratic and resource barriers to change by satisfying basic but unfulfilled human needs.
Outcomes	Produces a degree of predictability and order, and has the potential of consistently producing key results expected.	Produces change, often to a dramatic degree, and has the potential of producing particularly useful change (e.g. new approaches to a range of situations).

Source: Alan Hooper and John Potter, *Intelligent Leadership*, Random House, 2000

I would like to claim that there is a 'perfect' way of being a good team leader. Unfortunately, that is not the case. However, we can all become better at the role if we are open to learning and improving. The fun and challenging element of the role is that teams are made up of people and they provide the variety and stimulation to keep you from becoming complacent and allow you to continue to develop.

Chapter 2 What is a team?

There are differences between teams and groups in the workplace. Be clear about whether you are leading or managing a team or group. Although there are some similarities in what is required from you, there are some appreciable differences. Be careful you do not try to make a group function as a team, especially if it is not necessary. You run the risk of frustrating yourself if you treat the group as a team. The group is not interdependent to achieve their individual or collective outcomes. It is a better work environment if they get on, but it is not essential.

Recognise that all groups and teams move through the four stages from 'forming', through 'storming' on to 'norming' and then 'performing'. Remember the key characteristics of each stage. Think about what the team need from you to help them through the process – and adapt your style and approach. Take care that you do not stop the team at the 'storming' level because of possible conflict or disruption.

The type of team you are leading – work, project, focus or virtual – will need different things from you and will present you with a variety of challenges. Are you clear about which type of team and what they require from you?

Look back to Chapter 2 and think about the nine elements of effective teams. They are all important for your team. How well can you explain each one and what you do to apply it within your team? Which of these do you feel comfortable with managing and communicating? Where can you improve?

Chapter 3 Understanding team roles and balance

One of the key elements to understand when building and leading an effective team is to value difference. Too many inexperienced leaders, and even some who are experienced but ineffective, do not grasp this and put together a team made up of similar types of people and personalities. High-performing teams will comprise individuals who have clearly defined roles who can play to their strengths and appreciate the differences which their colleagues bring with their respective styles.

To help your team move through the group dynamics stages towards 'norming' and 'performing', make sure that each person has a clearly defined role so that they can understand what is expected of them and also know for what each team member is accountable. This is an important step. Not only does it provide structure and clarity for the team members; on the one hand it can help to prevent duplication of activities and responsibilities, on the other it can identify where gaps might occur for which no one is responsible.

Take time to read and understand the descriptions of the team roles as defined by Dr Meredith Belbin in Chapter 3. Identify your own preferred styles within these. At the same time, be aware of the styles which are not suitable for you. This is not an issue, you can get the balance within the team by finding some team members who can fulfil these roles. For example, if you are a natural 'resource investigator', 'shaper' and 'specialist' the team will benefit if you can encourage the 'co-ordinator', 'monitor-evaluator' and 'completer' roles within others.

As well as understanding your own preferred roles, you need to spend time assessing your team members and working out their preferred roles. It is fine to 'guess and test', i.e. 'guess' their role if you are not certain, and then 'test' by watching them within the team and observing whether they are behaving in line with that role. You can 'test' further by asking the individual to act in a specific way and notice whether they seem to be able to do it naturally, with some effort or not at all.

When you feel you have a clearer understanding of this it can be helpful to share your impressions with the team and get their input and thoughts. When there is a reasonable degree of common ground, you can encourage the team to explore the implications of the conclusions. What are their strengths as a team? What are the potential gaps? What can they do about these to compensate?

Having had this discussion, and drawing from the conclusions, your task is to make sure you capitalise on the strengths by utilising people's preferred roles. Look back at Chapter 3 and use some of the ideas in the 'Things to do' column from the table on pages 34–8.

Chapter 4 Your role as a leader

Leadership can be a tricky quality or behaviour to define. One person's experience of what they consider 'good leadership' might be another's 'too pushy' or 'too controlling' and another's 'too laid back'. At the end of the day, as a leader your challenge is to achieve results through others, while understanding that it is almost impossible to please all of the people all of the time.

Your confidence and competence as a leader can be influenced by the level at which you need to operate. When starting as a supervisor or first-line manager the emphasis is more about short-term activities and task achievement. Moving up, through middle management and overseeing departments or functions, there is a balance between the day-to-day performance and making sure it is working towards the overall strategy. As a senior manager or leader, or a business owner, you have to be able to think more long term in setting the vision and strategy to achieve this and you probably have to work with other managers who are responsible for the operational level (see Figure 10.1).

figure 10.1

You can develop up through the pyramid, as many will do. However, it is important to recognise where you can be most effective and which level suits your own style and your competencies. Moving on and getting out of your depth is not much use for you – or for your team. Good leadership is needed at all levels and it is equally important for teams at every level from the front line of the organisation through to the boardroom.

Although not an absolute divide, different leadership approaches can work more effectively at each level. Using a 'functional' leadership approach can be very effective at the team or task level. Figure 10.2 (overleaf) is the John Adair, Action Centred Leadership model described in Chapter 4.

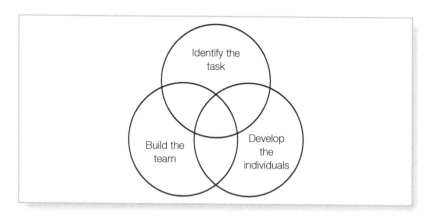

figure 10.2 From Adair, J., *Action-Centred Leadership* (Gower Publishing Ltd, 1979)

You need to pay attention to each of the three areas shown. Within these apply the specific functions:

- Defining the task
- Planning
- Briefing
- Controlling
- Evaluating
- Motivating
- Organising
- Providing examples.

Moving up the levels, the more 'behavioural' leadership models are likely to be more productive because you need to provide direction, support and development for the individuals who may also have to be role models and cascade the messages to their teams. Your team may well be leading their own teams too. Using 'Situational Leadership'® can be effective because it requires you to understand where your team members are on the maturity scale for each task and then choose the appropriate style from the four options to fit with this. Having a focused approach means you can work with team members in the way which is likely to suit where they are and means you are more likely to get the results you want.

Even if you are not feeling very comfortable about assuming the role, the people who are in your team will be looking to you to provide the leadership they need. This is especially the case if they are a new team or in the 'forming' or 'storming' stages. Be kind to yourself with your expectations and think about it as a learning process similar to learning to drive, playing a sport or a musical instrument. You do not start off perfect and the path is not always smooth or rapid. Learning to lead is similar. It might feel uncomfortable from the outset, and you may make some mistakes on the way. However, with practice and perseverance you will get better and your confidence will grow. A key difference is that when learning to drive, etc. you have an instructor or someone to guide you. When starting out as a leader, you usually have to teach yourself as you go.

Chapter 5 Setting the direction for your team

Your team do not only need you to provide leadership and to act as a leader, they will also want someone to give them an idea of the direction for the team and as individuals. Providing your team with a clear direction through effective goals and objectives can contribute to improved performance and motivation. The importance, power and benefits of goals and objectives apply to teams at all levels. Do not assume that if you are leading a senior or experienced team that this is not important for them.

Before setting goals for your team, check that you understand the bigger picture. Is there a clearly set vision? Whether this exists or not, are there clear goals and objective for the organisation? Are these shared so that you know what is expected of your team?

As the leader you need to make sure that the goals and objectives you set for your team are consistent with those set above you (if you are not running the organisation!) and that they fit with other departments or functions around you. Most of you will not be leading teams which operate in isolation.

When setting the goals and objectives remember you have several options for the process or model you want to use. To maximise their potential impact make sure that they are clear and specific. Think about the actual outcome the objective will deliver. Can it be defined and measured? If not, it is too vague and will not provide the motivation of a well set objective. Look back to Chapter 5 and remind yourself of the various choices for setting objectives and think about which ones you feel more comfortable with. You may want to consider which might work best with the different team members, or for various types of goal and objective. When setting the objectives, make sure you have agreement, not just acceptance.

Setting the direction is just the beginning. As the leader you do need to review them regularly to make sure that individuals or the team are on track and not slipping. This review process is as essential as setting the goal. There is little point in doing the initial phase if you do not keep a check on the progress.

Chapter 6 Monitoring and controlling performance

In some respects this is more of a management function than leadership. It might be thought of as less glamorous than many of the other elements of leadership. As I mentioned in the previous section, you need to review the progress towards all objectives as part of your monitoring and control. If you do not have the right elements in place to achieve this, the risk is that you, or the team, are likely to be out of control.

To monitor performance start by asking these questions (as mentioned in Chapter 6):

- What are the key activities I need to monitor?
- What are expected levels of performance for these?
- What evidence will I see, or need to see?
- How can I monitor them?
- How will the team report or communicate these activities?
- What actions will I take if we are not achieving the fundamental standards or are falling behind the plans?

To provide the core benchmark levels for monitoring make sure you establish the right KPIs (key performance indicators) or standards of performance. These provide a minimum acceptable level of performance. To be effective they should be: relevant, clear, fair, adaptable, respected.

When the team is new, or if they are underperforming, it is probably better that you set the KPIs. If they are more experienced and you are happy with their performance and attitude, I suggest you involve the team in establishing the areas and levels for them. This gets their buy in and commitment. You can set two types of KPI, quantitative (which have some numerical element to help with measurement) and qualitative (which will be more subjective or behavioural and need more thinking when arriving at a definition for acceptable performance). Most teams and roles will have a combination of the two.

These provide you with the foundation for your monitoring and control. They fit within the PEA model – Plan, Execution and After. You can monitor the 'execution' phase, and how well this is being done influences what you choose to do as part of the 'after'. They contribute towards the 'planning–control cycle' (see Figure 10.3).

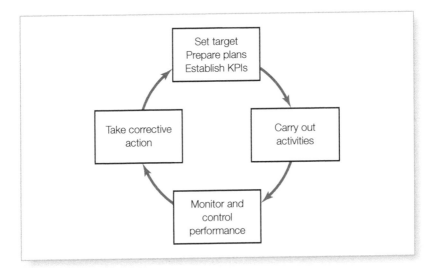

figure 10.3

The other part of this process is to identify other options for your control process. How can you monitor the intended or actual performance? When looking at this, think about how you can do it from as early a point as possible. It is simpler to take corrective action and get things back on track early on rather than just before expected completion dates.

Effective control systems need to be clear, simple and transparent. They should be beneficial for all concerned so that everyone knows how their performance is against plans and expectations. They might be written, based on discussion or observation or a combination of all these. Whatever you decide, the system needs to be consistent and fair.

Chapter 7 Communicating with your team

A quality which differentiates good leaders from the others is their communication ability. This involves more than whether they can make good presentations to the team and other groups. It is about how well they can connect with each team member on an individual basis and with the team as a whole when together. How effectively can they put across their messages and, even more importantly, how well do they listen and respond to people?

Unfortunately, communication is something many people take for granted and rarely think about. This is one of the reasons why so many communication errors occur, leading to misunderstandings and more. I believe that this is one area where any one of us can improve with a bit of thought and effort. Taking a bit of time to think about what we want to 'send' and how can help us improve the effectiveness of our message. Developing flexibility in how we communicate and interact can only help. Deciding to be more focused when we listen will make people enjoy interacting with us and appreciate the fact we are paying attention to them. You can practise this in all areas of your life, not just at work.

When thinking about communicating, consider the definition 'To understand and to be understood' and what it means. From here, ask the key questions before sending any message:

Why am I communicating?

Who is the receiver?

What is the message? (And my objective?)

How should I communicate?

How can I get feedback?

Spending a few minutes thinking through these might make a significant difference to the effectiveness of your message. The more you do this, the better you will become.

Another reason for working at your communication is that you will be a role model for your team, and other colleagues. They will look to you and how you communicate and behave and this provides the lead for what is considered good or acceptable communication within the team. Be clear with your messages, use the appropriate channel and, if face to face, be aware of your body language and the signals that it might send. Encourage two-way communication and reinforce this through engaged listening and allowing people to finish what they are saying without you interrupting.

These behaviours can become the acceptable standard within your team if you demonstrate them often enough. Whether team members are interacting with each other in their day-to-day work or in team meetings, they can adopt these communication behaviours. This will lead to a better working environment and better relationships, which should support improved morale and performance.

Chapter 8 Getting the most from your team

This is one area which can be either very satisfying when you get it right, whether for an individual or the team as a whole, or extremely frustrating or demoralising when you cannot seem to get through to them. There is no one simple solution or method which will work all of the time with all of the people. (Leadership would be much easier if there was!) This is why it can be such a challenge for leaders. Your team members will each have their own set of needs, attitudes, issues, wishes and skills which can keep changing weekly, daily or more frequently. The combination of these factors will influence what they need to make them motivated at that time. It is this which catches out many leaders, because they do not necessarily adapt their approach to fit with the individual. Another limitation for many leaders is that they have a tendency to address motivating their team in line with what they feel motivates themselves.

Motivation is about encouraging or getting movement. In Chapter 8, I covered a number of theories or approaches and I suggest you make sure you are familiar with them. You do not have to be an expert on all of them. Some will seem to make more sense to you than others, or will feel more comfortable. These will be the ones you can use more easily with your team now and in the future. No particular motivational theory or model works better than any other. There are some common themes though. Longer-term motivation which is deeper and more long lasting is usually 'intrinsic'. It will be generated from within when various internal triggers operate. As a leader, you cannot necessarily make this happen. What you can do is provide the climate where the triggers can be stimulated. Too many leaders think that they need to motivate their team members through 'extrinsic' factors. These tend to be the carrot and stick ideas, or rewards and punishments. They can have a place occasionally but they will usually only produce a short-term result. Their impact will wear off quickly. Another problem is that the carrot becomes the norm, so you need to keep finding bigger and better ones. The stick does not generate motivation, it just generates a behaviour of avoidance, doing just enough to avoid the pain.

When thinking about motivating your team members, your responsibility is not necessarily to be the motivator. I believe that you need to understand the principles, understand what contributes to the intrinsic motivation of your team members, create the right climate for these factors to thrive – and avoid demotivating your people. If you pay attention to this you will get more from them.

You can also get more by thinking about developing the team members. If you have established the right climate, most of your people will want to improve their job skills and competencies, and many will also be open to personal development. You can support this in a number of ways. Using formal training is one option but is only part of the way forward. The workplace gives many opportunities to encourage the team to learn and grow. Giving people responsibility for specific projects can be beneficial. Delegating tasks to individuals can be productive (and helps your time management). This is giving someone responsibility for the task in a controlled manner, with freedom to get on with it while having some checks built in, and then reviewing at the end to see what has been learned. It is not just 'dumping' the task on an individual.

Where you can make a significant contribution to people's development is through coaching. Do not be put off by thinking you cannot do this. The notes in Chapter 8 offer you some guidelines and approaches to use. It does not have to be complicated. Identify areas for improvement and from here it is mainly about using good communication skills, especially questioning and listening. The key is to get the individual to come up with ideas and options for how they can tackle the issue and arrive at their own preferred solution. Your role is to offer a combination of support and challenge through your questions. From here you can reinforce the learning, and contribute to their motivation, by giving effective, constructive feedback.

Chapter 9 Handling challenges within the team

Whether your team is at the 'forming' stage or it has reached 'performing', it can still provide challenges for you because of the way people interact and behave. Too many inexperienced or ineffective leaders either overlook or ignore these challenges, or hope they will smooth over and go away. Unfortunately, they rarely do and these issues severely limit the team's performance.

You do not want to have either of the extremes within your team. When it appears to be too smooth and harmonious, with everyone in agreement, it is not necessarily a good thing. Although it might seem to be an ideal scenario, the danger is that 'groupthink' is happening, where the emphasis is on harmony and avoiding disagreement. The drawback is that ideas are rarely challenged or explored in any depth. At the other end, you do not want constant friction and disagreement. This leads to a lack of effective communication with people not wanting to work with each other and becoming demotivated.

There is a middle ground which can be positive. Effective teams will have an openness in their communication and way of working. They recognise that it is a good thing to discuss and debate ideas and how they are operating. They will develop ways of achieving this which are constructive. As the leader you can help towards this by encouraging these behaviours. Appreciate that conflict does not have to be a negative behaviour if it is handled properly. Whether it is an issue between individuals or a wider one within the team, people can learn to handle these disagreements in a more positive way. Introduce them to the principles of the conflict handling approaches outlined in Chapter 9 and guide them through the steps.

Where the challenges are showing as communication breakdowns or personality clashes with team members you can play a part in tackling them. The key is to step in as early as you can before the situation escalates to a point of no return. Be a good mediator by behaving calmly and objectively. Allow each side to express their understanding of things and how and why they have reached these conclusions. Focus on the desired outcome and act non-judgementally to work towards a positive resolution and way ahead.

It is important to remember that a high-performing team will have challenges; at times there might appear to be conflict and disagreements. What differentiates them as a high-performing team is how they deal with these issues, with the support of their leader, and go back to focusing on achieving their goals and objectives. They do not avoid the issues, nor does their leader.

Exercises

Chapter 2 What is a team?

Think about the different stages of the group dynamics process and answer the following for each one:

■ What are the typical behaviours or characteristics of the stage? How should you approach leading the team at each stage?

Forming:

Storming:

Norming:

Performing:

■ What type of team are you leading? Work, project, focus or virtual? What are the differences between each?

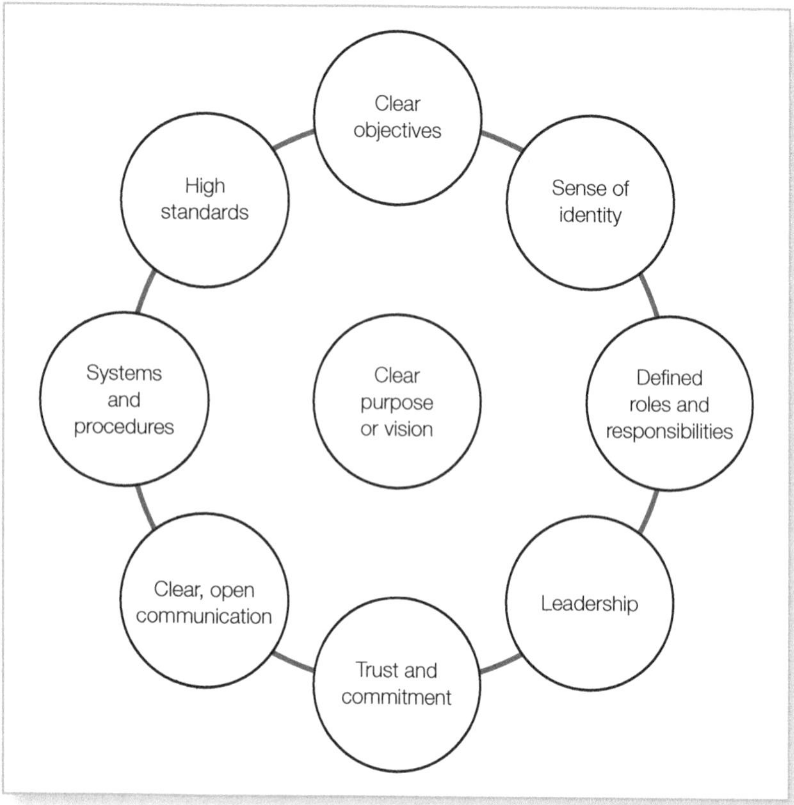

figure 10.4

- Look at each of the nine elements of an effective team shown in Figure 10.4. How well do you think these are defined and in place with your team?
- Ask the team members what they feel about each one and whether it can be improved.

Chapter 3 Understanding team roles and balance

Think about your team members and assess who fits each group: Doers, Thinkers, Carers, etc. Can you place them in the appropriate category? What makes you feel this? How can you make the most of them within the team by utilising this knowledge more effectively?

Revisit the exercise below and notice where the gaps are, and where there might be a number of people with the same preferred roles. Think about how you can handle these.

List the team members on the left and then indicate the roles:

Team role / Name	Plant	Resource investigator	Co-ordinator	Shaper	Monitor evaluator	Team worker	Implementer	Completer	Specialist

Preferred role ✓   Possible role ?   Avoid ✗

Chapter 4 Your role as a leader

How would you rate yourself against each of these qualities? What can you do to improve each one?

Integrity:

Positive:

Determined:

Sincere:

Sensitive:

Toughness:

Humility:

Warmth:

Communication:

Developer:

Take time to look back at the elements of functional leadership and assess how comfortable you are with each one, and how effective you are. How can you improve where you need to?

- Defining the task
- Planning
- Briefing
- Controlling
- Evaluating
- Motivating
- Organising
- Providing examples.

Chapter 5 Setting the direction for your team

Set three objectives for yourself, either relating to work and your team or personal. Use at least two of the methods in Chapter 5, SMARTER, one-minute objective setting, or stepping up and stepping down.

1

2

3

Remember to do an action plan to help you achieve the objective if you need more detail.

Chapter 6 Monitoring and controlling performance

If you have not done this already, create a list of key performance indicators or standards of performance for your team. Do both quantitative and qualitative ones. When you have your list, discuss it with the team and be open to making any adjustments based on their input and suggestions. Once you have an agreed list, I suggest you publish and circulate it so that everyone has a copy.

Chapter 7 Communicating with your team

How open are you to getting feedback? A good way of improving your communication is to ask some people to tell you how effective you are when you are the 'sender'. What could you improve?

Before team meetings or dealing with any individual, practise using the following five questions:

Why am I communicating?

Who is the receiver?

What is the message? (And my objective?)

How should I communicate?

How can I get feedback?

Develop your listening skills by focusing on the speaker. Give them your full attention, look at them and resist any temptation to interrupt them or jump to what you want to say.

Chapter 8 Getting the most from your team

Spend some time thinking about each of your team members. Can you identify what might be their drivers in terms of intrinsic motivators? What do they seem to respond to? What do they seem to be concerned about or worry about?

For each person note what you think might be the answers to these questions. Then look at the different concepts of motivation and identify the ones you feel most comfortable with. Using these, choose some ideas for how you might be able to apply them with each individual and note them down.

Now test these ideas out with each person. If any do not seem to work at first, try again. After two or three goes, look back at your notes and reconsider whether you might have the wrong drivers, or whether it is the wrong approach. Either way, it is not a problem. Re-evaluate and then choose a different option and keep going until you find a combination that works. Having done this, do not assume it stays the same. The individual's drivers and needs might change, which means you have to adjust your approach.

To develop your coaching, look for opportunities to coach. It can also help you to find someone who can coach you so that you experience the process. When starting coaching I suggest you keep it simple and use the ROAR process (Having said this, feel free to try out the GROW model too. Examples of some questions for each process are at the end of the chapter).

Handling challenges within the team

It is not necessary to create a conflict situation just to practise the ideas in this chapter. However, you might find some circumstances in other areas of your life where you can test out the conflict handling strategies. Keep your eyes and ears open for opportunities and step in and have a go at resolving whatever the issue is. I do not recommend that you look to set up situations.

My personal action plan

To help you identify what you have learned from this book and to assess where you still want to develop, revisit the questionnaire, from Chapter 1, below. Read each statement or question and assess your current level of skill or knowledge for it.

0–1   Don't know, no real knowledge, don't do this.

2–3   Some awareness, some knowledge, do sometimes, could be better.

4–5   Comfortable with this, think I am competent or good at it (though not complacent!).

When you have scored each group of statements/questions, identify some specific action or outcome you want to achieve for it. Pay particular attention to those items which you have scored between 0 and 3.

No.	Item	Rating	Notes
1	How well do you know the characteristics of an effective team?		
2	Can you describe what types of team you currently lead?		
3	Are you able to recognise the different stages a team goes through as it develops?		

Objective/action:

No.	Item	Rating	Notes
4	What types of roles are required for a well-balanced team?		
5	Can you identify the preferred roles of your team members?		
6	How well do you recognise the benefits of having differences between the team members and their styles, rather than too much similarity?		

Objective/action:

No.	Item	Rating	Notes
7	How comfortable are you with leading people?		
8	Do you feel you should change your leadership style with your team or for individuals?		
9	Do you understand your role and responsibilities as a leader?		

Objective/action:

No.	Item	Rating	Notes
10	How important is it for the team to have clear goals?		
11	How will you make sure individuals have their own objectives to achieve?		
12	Have you identified areas to set standards of performance or key performance indicators?		

No.	Item	Rating	Notes

Objective/action:

13	Do you have processes or systems in place for monitoring the team's performance?		
14	Are you willing to act quickly when you see things slipping (collectively or with individuals)?		
15	What could you do to involve the team members in monitoring performance? Would you be happy to do so?		

Objective/action:

16	How well do you communicate with the team?		
17	How comfortable are you dealing with people face to face?		
18	Could you improve communication within the team?		

Objective/action:

19	Do you consciously look for opportunities to coach team members and to develop their skills?		
20	How good are you at 'catching 'em doing something right' and giving praise?		
21	Do you know what type of recognition or acknowledgement will work best for each of your team members?		

Objective/action:

22	Do you prefer to avoid or prevent conflict within the team?		
23	How well do you understand the dangers of 'groupthink'?		
24	How comfortable are you at addressing and handling conflict within the team?		

Objective/action:

Identify three to five areas to set your own objectives and action plans to develop your leadership skills with a team. For each area, describe what you want to achieve, what the end outcome will be, what steps you will take to get there and where you might get help or support if needed.

1

2

3

4

5

'ROAR' coaching – some ideas for questions to help you

The questions shown are only indicators and you do not have to use all of them in each step!

Right now:

- What has to be done to........? and why?
- What do think of the way you ....?
- What could you do differently/better?
- What would you like to be able to achieve?
- What do you think is the reason for........?
- What does your instinct say you could do?
- What result did you get when you........? Was that what you wanted?
- What are the challenges you have with doing........?   What problems does that give you?

Options:

- What else could you do?
- What other ways do you think you could........?
- How else could you.....?
- What ideas do you have for......?
- What other things do you need to consider?
- Which option do you think would give you the best results?
- Do you want me to suggest some options?
- What would you see as the advantages and disadvantages of each option?
- On a scale of 1–10, how attractive is each option?

Action:

- What steps do you need to take?
- What will you do first?
- What might stop you?...........What can you do about it?

Now step back and observe. Compare the behaviour and outcomes with what was discussed and agreed. (And give time and space for the person to complete the task.)

Review:

- How do you feel that went?
- What went well? Why do you think that was?
- What could have gone better? Why do you think that was?
- What will you do differently next time?
- What have you learned from this?
- What could prevent you being successful next time? How will you overcome this?
- What other support or help do you need from me, or others?

The 'GROW' Model – questions to help

Goal
- What is it that you want from this discussion?
- What do you want to achieve long-term and short term?
- What will be happening when you have achieved your goal?
- What will have changed when you are successful?
- What would be your ideal outcome?
- When do you want to achieve it?

Reality
- What is happening now?
- Who is involved?
- What have you done about this so far?
- What results did that produce?
- What are the main blocks to finding a way forward?
- What has helped so far?

Options
- What ideas do you have?
- What else could you do?
- What might work?
- What if you were to...?
- How about the suggestion...?
- What would you gain from doing that?
- Who else might help you?

Will
- What are you going to do?
- When will you do that?
- How will that help you?
- What can you do to overcome that?
- What support do you need?
- What will help you to stay on track?
- How will you keep going?

On a scale of 1–10 what is the likelihood of you taking that action?

Index

FINANCIAL TIMES
Essential Guides

9780273761136

9780273757986

9780273757993

9780273768135

9780273772217

9780273772422

Available to buy online and from all good bookshops
www.pearson-books.com